Fiachra Ó Ceallaigh, ofm.
Rinn Mhic Ghormáin

READING – WHICH APPROACH?

Reading - which approach?

Vera Southgate and Geoffrey R. Roberts

 University of London Press Ltd

ISBN 0 340 11852 0 Unibook

University of London Press Ltd
St Paul's House, Warwick Lane, London EC4P 4AH
Photographs by Henry Grant, AIIP
Printed in Great Britain by
Hazell Watson and Viney Ltd, Aylesbury, Bucks

Contents

ACKNOWLEDGEMENTS

The authors wish to express grateful thanks to Mr C. Hully and the staff of Lane End County Primary School, Cheadle Hulme, and to Miss E. L. Gourlay and the staff of Old Moat Infants School, Manchester, for their valuable help and co-operation over the taking of photographs for this book.

The authors and publishers wish to acknowledge Educational Explorers Ltd, Reading, Berks, for the colour charts from *Words in Colour* by C. Gattegno (between pages 152 and 153), and Thomas Nelson & Sons Ltd, London, for two extracts from *Colour Story Reading* by J. K. Jones (pages 2 and 3 of the colour inset between pages 152 and 153).

Some aspects of the subject of this book have been discussed by Mrs Southgate in a paper entitled 'The Problem of Selecting an Approach to the Teaching of Reading' which was read to the Second Annual Conference of the United Kingdom Reading Association at London University in July 1965, and which was later published in Downing, J. A. and Brown, A. L. (eds.) (1967) *The Second International Reading Symposium.* London: Cassell, and thanks are also due to the publishers of this work.

PART ONE
Aims and Terminology

PLEASE NOTE   The names of authors mentioned in the text are usually followed by the dates of publication of their books, which are listed in the Bibliography (pages 201–6). Where an author has had more than one book published in a year, it is categorized as for example, (1967a) or (1967b).

1 The purpose of this book

The main aim of this book is to help teachers and student teachers to find an answer to one practical question which they frequently ask: namely, which reading books and equipment they should use in their schools and classes. In particular, the book is concerned with the selection of approaches for the early stages of learning to read.

This represents a very real problem to teachers, and its importance is accentuated by the high priority which they give to the acquisition of the skill of reading. It is their belief in the importance of reading which causes most teachers in primary schools, special schools, the slower streams of secondary modern schools and remedial classes to be so anxious to help children to read as easily and speedily as possible. Yet, however good the work these teachers are doing, they are rarely entirely satisfied with the reading progress of their pupils. Accordingly, most of them tend to look hopefully, not only at newly published reading schemes, but also at new media and other ideas on reading which are constantly appearing.

It is at this point that the reading teacher finds herself* faced with a dilemma. Attendance at lectures, as well as the study of books, articles and advertisements describing new approaches to reading and new reading equipment reveal an increasing range of ideas, each being advanced as a universal remedy for children's failure to make satisfactory reading progress. The authors and originators of the new ideas, often supported by those teachers who first experiment with the new materials and techniques, generally claim spectacular results. One would not wish to suggest that the claims made by authors and enthusiastic practitioners are false; on the contrary, one can whole-heartedly believe in these results – in all of them!

* For the sake of clarity, throughout this book the teacher is referred to as feminine, and the child as masculine.

For it is vital to remember that most ways of teaching reading work extremely well in the hands of the originators, who are likely to bring enthusiasm and drive to the utilization of their innovations.

The effect of these glowing reports of children's reading progress resulting from the introduction of innovations, is frequently to make teachers dissatisfied with their own efforts in this field. There is a tendency for them to feel that if they neglect to adopt a new scheme or approach to reading, they may be failing to do their best for their pupils. The problem faced by teachers in these circumstances is one of selection. When the various new ways of teaching reading all appear to accelerate children's progress, how can teachers choose?

Although the practising teacher may be interested in a general way in what authors and experimenters have achieved by using new approaches to reading, her own interest in new ideas is more specific. She wants to know how a particular innovation might be likely to benefit the children in her own class. Although an apparently straightforward question, this is actually a complicated one with many subtle undertones. There can be no one definite answer and certainly there is no one formula which lends itself to general application. On the other hand, merely to point out that the selection of an ideal way of helping children to read depends on innumerable factors – however true this may be – is of little assistance to the questioning teacher. The issue is further clouded by the similarity of the rival claims for the many new ideas on reading now being advocated.

It would, however, be unfortunate if the difficulty of judging between different ways of learning to read caused teachers to eschew new ideas, and so cling solely to methods and books with which they were familiar. Advances in education have tended to develop from the work of those who are willing to experiment. Moreover, there is generally one advantage to be gained by experimenting with any new means of teaching reading, in that its use tends to act as a stimulant to the teacher and, through her, on the children who are learning to read.

In this book no attempt is made to answer the teacher's question by suggesting that one approach to reading is 'the best'. The aim is rather to consider some of the factors which influence the choice and to suggest certain principles of selection which can help the teacher to reach her own decision. Two points should perhaps be stressed at this stage. Firstly, it is unlikely that any one way of teaching reading will prove equally effective for *all* pupils, taught by *all* teachers, in *all* classes or schools. Secondly, research results which supply us with definite answers on the merits of different approaches are just not available. Moreover, many of the published results are conflicting. For example, Chall (1967) in her book, *Learning to Read: The Great Debate**, reporting her own large piece of research in which she analysed sixty-seven different research studies which compared different approaches to beginning reading, mentions the conclusions of a special committee held in 1959 on this very subject. The committee's conclusions were that 'the research then available provided evidence so vague, contradictory and incomplete as to encourage conflicting interpretations. No serious researcher could state with any degree of certainty, on the basis of such evidence, that either one or another approach to beginning reading was indeed the best or the worst.' The situation could be described in exactly the same words today.

A teacher's decision regarding the way in which children should learn to read is usually crystallised in the ordering of appropriate reading books and equipment for her class. Accordingly, the basic issue pursued throughout this book leads inevitably to the selection of reading materials. It will be shown that the choice of materials depends as much on the beliefs and aims of the teacher as on her preferred method of reading tuition and the working conditions within the school.

It may be that those teachers in whose classes learning to read springs almost entirely from the children's own individual activities, with a reliance on hand-made apparatus and books, augmented by large collections of individual books, will find the theme of the book of less interest than those teachers who prefer to centre reading activities, even to a limited extent, on a chosen reading scheme or approach.

The book is likely to prove most useful to head teachers and teachers who are considering the possibility of altering the approach to reading currently in use in their schools. It might also prove helpful to teachers who are not considering making major changes involving the purchase of new materials as the ideas developed may suggest ways in which the maximum benefits can be gained by using the reading materials already in their schools.

* For a bibliographical reference list of all books mentioned in the text see pages 201–6.

The fact that the authors are attempting to lay down some guide-lines for teachers on the selection of reading materials should not be taken to imply that they consider the choice of materials to be the most important factor in the beginning reading programmes. Indeed, they are of the opinion that other factors frequently have much greater influence on the ways in which children learn to read than does the selection of appropriate materials. Nevertheless, because this is a practical question with which teachers are constantly concerned, the authors believe that it merits serious consideration. It is hoped that this book, by setting out a few basic principles of selection designed to encourage teachers to formulate their own answers to the question of 'Which approach?', might contribute to a more careful appraisal of new reading materials and other innovations prior to their adoption.

ONE SUGGESTION FOR FURTHER READING

Those teachers who wish to study in greater depth some of the philosophical bases upon which will rest their decisions about teaching methods will find guidance in:

DEARDEN, R. F. (1968) *The Philosophy of Primary Education.* London: Routledge and Kegan Paul.

Among other things Dearden discusses are: the aims of the curriculum, the place of activity, play and experience in the learning processes, and the role and the tasks of the teacher in the school.

2 Terminology

Many different words and phrases are currently being used to describe identical factors relating to the acquisition of the skill of reading while, conversely, certain words are being given a variety of meanings by different people. It is clearly important that any book concerned with reading should begin by defining precisely the terminology to be used. Thus, in order to avoid confusion and possible misunderstandings, the following terms are used throughout this book according to the definitions and descriptions given.

A. METHOD

The word 'method' is the one most familiar to teachers. In the literature on the teaching of reading, and likewise in practice, it has tended to be used in a rather narrow sense to represent two different ways of commencing reading tuition. On the one hand are what Gray (1956) describes as 'global methods', in which whole words or sentences are considered as the initial basic units. In the everyday phraseology of teachers and most educators, global methods are usually referred to as either look-and-say word method or look-and-say sentence method, depending on whether separate words or complete sentences are considered as the initial learning units. On the other hand, there are the 'phonic methods' in which the initial emphasis is on the letters, digraphs and syllables which form regular words. When the method begins with individual letters and sounds which are then combined to form words, it is termed a 'synthetic' phonic method. If it begins with regular words, which are analysed into their component sounds and written symbols, it is called an 'analytic' phonic method.

In practice, the irregularity of English spelling has been partially responsible for leading the majority of teachers to employ both methods, in what is usually termed an 'eclectic approach' to reading. The main variations are generally represented by the selection of one of these methods for use in the initial stages, and the timing of the introduction of the other method in the reading programme.

Accordingly, although the word 'method' has a wider connotation in everyday language, it is used throughout this book in the narrower, but professionally accepted sense, to refer to 'look-and-say' methods, 'phonic' methods or a combination of both.

B. MEDIUM

The word 'medium' first entered common usage in the field of reading some ten years ago when Pitman (1959) introduced his Augmented Roman Alphabet (A.R.A.). 'Medium' is a term used for the actual form of written or printed symbols employed to represent our spoken language. Prior to 1959 few teachers had considered the possibility of employing any other medium than that which is now referred to as 't.o.'. This is the accepted abbreviation for 'traditional orthography', which merely refers to the normal usage of our twenty-six-letter alphabet when it is employed according to the accepted rules of the English spelling system. The Augmented Roman Alphabet was later renamed The Initial Teaching Alphabet and is now generally referred to by its abbreviation of 'i.t.a.' (see illustrated example on page 182).

In addition, media currently being used, or considered for use, for beginning reading include colour codes (see colour inset between pages 152–3), and the addition to t.o. of various systems of differentiating marks. The latter, which are usually termed 'diacritical marks', can take the form of strokes through silent letters, lines above vowels which have long sounds, and so on (see illustrated example on page 47).

C. MATERIALS

The medium chosen to represent the written form of the spoken language is utilised in the preparation of all sorts of reading materials designed to help children to learn to read. The term 'reading materials' is used in this book to mean not only basic reading schemes with all their supporting supplementary books, apparatus, games, pictures and so on, but also other printed books and publications of all kinds, as well as hand-written cards, labels, lists, charts, stories and every form of written letters and words.

D. PROCEDURE

The manner in which the selected reading materials, based on a particular method and printed in the chosen medium, are utilized within any class contributes to the development of a pattern of active processes directly affecting reading progress. The following factors are among those discernible within this pattern: the grouping of children for reading activities; the formality or informality of the instruction or learning situations; the timing of the commencement of reading tuition and the manner in which it is undertaken; the total time devoted to reading and supportive activities, as well as the way in which reading spreads over into other subjects or is treated in comparative isolation; and the extent and variety of the reading materials themselves and their availability to the children.

The phrase 'classroom procedure' is suggested as a suitable, comprehensive term to represent the totality of all these dynamic processes affecting children's reading progress.

E. APPROACH

The phrase 'approach to reading' has recently been used in a variety of ways without acquiring any accepted definition. In different contexts it has been employed to mean a method, a medium, a reading scheme or a set of equipment. Yet, the acceptance of the phrase into common use in the field of reading probably arose in the search for an appropriate general phrase which did not denote specifically either method or medium.

In this book the phrase 'approach to reading' is being used in a general sense rather than being equated with any one factor in the reading situation. It usually implies a combination of certain of the factors – frequently 'the three m's', in which a selected medium and method are utilized in the production of particular reading materials.

ONE SUGGESTION FOR FURTHER READING

A more detailed description of the terms used in this chapter can be found
in:

SOUTHGATE, V. (1968b) 'Formulae for beginning reading tuition'.
Educational Research, **11**, 23–30.

PART TWO
Criteria for Assessing Reading Approaches

3 Factors influencing reading progress

1. The Multiplicity of Factors

There are so many factors which can influence children's reading progress
that a much larger book than the present one would be required to consider them all in detail. Yet the teacher selecting an approach to reading
must have some awareness of the multiplicity of these factors. A mere list
of influential factors is unlikely to provide useful guide-lines in this context. On the other hand, a broad grouping of factors may help to structure
the pattern of influences and serve to illustrate that in each different
approach there is an emphasis on the vital importance of certain factors,
often to the neglect of other factors considered to be less influential.

Four broad groups of factors affecting the acquisition of reading skills
are suggested relating to: the task itself and the ways in which it may be
mastered; the learner; the teacher; and the situation in which the learning
takes place.

A. THE TASK

One group of factors concerns the nature of the task itself, definitions of the
skill of reading and beliefs and theories about how this task may be
mastered. When the task consists of reading printed and written English,
the alphabet employed and the complexity or simplicity of the accepted
rules of English spelling represent important factors in the situation, as do
the rules of grammar and the common usage of words and phrases in our
spoken language.

What one understands by 'learning to read' and, consequently, what one is aiming at, introduces other factors into this group. We find that different authorities on the teaching of reading differ in the emphases they place on the various stages of learning to read. For example, Fries (1962) places his emphasis on decoding in the very early stages, Daniels and Diack (1957) emphasise the structure of the word, while Obrist and Pickard (1967) stress the unity of the sentence. It is quite clear that these authors hold different views on the nature of the task itself, as well as on the way in which it might best be mastered.

Beliefs about the nature of reading are likely to lead to different practices for beginning reading tuition and so are the various learning theories proposed by psychologists. Each practice constitutes a new set of influential factors. Perhaps even more important is the fact that the manner in which tuition commences may not only spring from beliefs about the nature of reading, but may in itself be a potent factor affecting the kind of reading which results from the tuition. R. Morris (1963), for example, suggests that if children were encouraged to make more active and personal responses to the text of their early reading materials, they would be likely to develop into more thoughtful readers.

B. THE LEARNER

A second group of factors relates to the learner – the individual child who faces the task of learning to read the English language. In every class there will be certain factors common to some, if not all, of the children and other factors which are unique to individual children. The personal factors are more likely to show greater variations than the social factors between children in the same group or class.

Personal factors likely to influence children's reading progress include physical, intellectual, emotional and personality characteristics. At a physical level, age, health, amount of sleep, eye-sight, hearing and hand and eye dominance may all be influential. Intelligence has long been accepted as closely correlated with reading attainment, as has emotional development. At a personality level, interest, motivation, persistence and preferred way of working all have bearing on learning to read.

Among the relevant factors in the child's social background are the socio-economic and cultural levels of his parents, including their interest in books and the extent to which they read, and their interest in the child's school progress. Wiseman (1967) for instance, in *The Manchester Survey* which he carried out for the Plowden Committee, found that his analysis 'underlined the importance of the home background as a determinant of the educational progress and attainment of primary-school children'. Furthermore, he noted that 'family literacy, as evinced by measures of reading and library membership', proved to be one of the most significant factors.

C. THE TEACHER

Just as each child is unique, so is each teacher. Both personal and social differences distinguish teachers from each other although, because of the selection procedures through which they have passed, there is likely to be a smaller range of differences between teachers than between children. Nevertheless, teachers differ not only in physical characteristics such as age and health but also in personality, in ability, in training and in teaching experience. Also, a teacher's innate characteristics combined with her training and experience have led her to form certain opinions about education, about children and about reading. Her thoughts on these subjects cause her to believe in certain methods, to prefer certain classroom procedures and perhaps to have formed rigid habits of teaching reading. All these factors relating to the teacher have a great effect on her choice of a reading approach and ultimately on the reading attainments of her pupils.

D. THE SITUATION

The teacher who is helping the child to master the task of learning to read is doing so in a particular situation. Numerous factors present in this situation are related both directly and indirectly to the teacher's choice of an approach to reading. Among the broader background features of the reading environment should be listed the type of school or educational institution in which the reading is to take place and the area in which it is situated. At a closer level, physical features of the actual space in which the learning will be undertaken, such as the size of the room, the furniture and fitments and the space available for the movement of children are all relevant. The number of other children present in the teaching–learning situation, and the ways in which they resemble or differ from the child in question, also represent important factors in the environment. But the situation which represents the teaching–learning unit is not merely an inanimate backcloth made up of room, furniture and other children, in front of which teacher and child concentrate on the task. The 'climate of the school' and the beliefs of the teacher combine to produce, within this physical environment, a definite pattern of procedures. Thus a dynamic situation, of which the teacher, the learner and the task are integral parts, comes into existence. Accordingly, not only the separate features of the environment but also their interactions within this dynamic situation constitute important factors influencing children's reading progress.

2. Three Practical Decisions

All the foregoing factors, among others, are considered to affect children's reading progress in varying degrees and must, therefore, be relevant to the selection of reading materials. Yet it is not suggested that it is possible for a head teacher or teacher to pay meticulous attention to every one of these factors. Indeed, to the teacher selecting a new approach to reading, many of these factors are so much part of her background knowledge of the children in her class that she hardly thinks consciously of them. Consequently, certain approaches are never seriously considered as possibilities but are discarded, out of hand.

Accordingly, the aim of this book is not to develop all the strands which may ultimately contribute to an appropriate choice of reading materials but rather to concentrate on a few important criteria. In so doing, a developmental plan for the selection of reading materials is proposed, which will enable the teacher progressively to narrow the field of choice and so arrive at an approach well suited to her own and the children's needs.

This plan, which must necessarily be related to the totality of factors influencing reading progress, involves the teacher in making three main decisions, in a specified order. The first decision, which might appear to be of a theoretical nature but is actually an extremely practical point, concerns a teacher's basic beliefs about the way in which children can best be introduced to the skill of reading. The second decision, which can only be taken in the light of the first decision, concerns methods and media. Only when these two questions have been answered, will the teacher be in a strong position to reach the third decision regarding specific approaches. The teacher who makes these three decisions, in this order, will be likely to find a satisfactory answer to the question, 'Which approach to reading?'

SUGGESTIONS FOR FURTHER READING

A detailed analysis of the nature of reading can be found in the following publications:

CLYMER, T. (1968) 'What is "reading"?: some current concepts.' In ROBINSON, H. M. (ed.) *Innovation and Change in Reading Instruction.* The Sixty-seventh Yearbook of the National Society for the Study of Education, Part 2. Chicago: Chicago University Press.

DIACK, H. (1960) *Reading and the Psychology of Perception.* Nottingham: Skinner.

ROBERTS, G. R. (1969) *Reading in Primary Schools.* London: Routledge & Kegan Paul.

ROBERTS, G. R. and LUNZER, E. A. (1968) 'Reading and learning to read.' In LUNZER, E. A. and MORRIS, J. F. *Development in Human Learning.* London: Staples.

There is a great deal written about the learner in:

DEPARTMENT OF EDUCATION AND SCIENCE (1967) The Plowden Report: *Children and their Primary Schools,* Vol. 1. London: H.M. Stationery Office;

and there are some interesting facts about the teacher of reading in:

GOODACRE, E. J. (1968) *Teachers and their Pupils' Home Background.*
   Slough: N.F.E.R.

Research evidence on the impact of the school situation upon children's
reading progress is given in:

MORRIS, J. M. (1966) *Standards and Progress in Reading.* Slough: N.F.E.R.

Further details of the influence of both the school and the home environment on children's scholastic progress can be found in the following
publications:

WISEMAN, S. (1964) *Education and Environment.* Manchester: Manchester
   University Press.

DEPARTMENT OF EDUCATION AND SCIENCE (1967) The Plowden Report:
   Children and their Primary Schools, Vol. 2. Appendices 9, 10 and 11,
   pp. 347–594. London: H.M. Stationery Office.

4. The first decision –
incidental or systematic teaching?

1. Two Contrasting Beliefs

The first decision which a teacher should make before selecting an approach to reading represents a choice between two main beliefs about how children may best be helped to learn to read. Those holding one belief regard reading principally as a skill to be taught, while supporters of the alternative belief are more concerned with how the skill may be learnt. Certain teachers may quibble with the suggested dichotomy between teaching and learning, indicating that they are complementary processes and are frequently found in operation together. While this is true, there is nevertheless a fundamental difference between the beliefs of those who favour teaching the skill of reading and those whose emphases are on learning.

The first teacher, who may be described as a systematic teacher-leader, believes that both instruction and learning require planning in advance in definite stages which form a systematic progression. She is more likely to structure the learning situations to fit in with the overall plan of developmental tuition than to leave children free to learn to read in a relatively unstructured situation.

The systematic teacher considers learning to read to be of prime importance to the young child. She does not want to curtail his other interests, which she may well consider to be of great value, but rather to place reading as top priority. Such a teacher, when putting forward her views on reading will be likely to speak in the following terms: 'I firmly believe that it is important to teach the child to read in the infant school.

Reading is the basic skill. Once the child has mastered reading, he has the key to so many other subjects. This is why I pay great attention to reading.'

The second teacher, who may be termed a teacher-counsellor or teacher-consultant lays much less emphasis on teaching and more on the provision of an environment in which children can be expected to learn to read. She may do a certain amount of direct teaching but it is more likely to arise incidentally than to form part of a systematic plan including both teaching and learning processes. She believes that most children will learn to read in an appropriate school environment; that is, an environment which provides them with security and considers the all-round development of each individual child. The school environment will be filled with a wide variety of stimuli and will extend beyond the boundaries of the classroom. The child will be encouraged to explore and experiment, to discover things for himself and to participate in interesting experiences with other children. Speech and written language will be considered important and an abundance of different kinds of books and materials for creative work will be freely available to the children. The Ministry of Education (1959) described such an environment as one 'in which the skills of reading and writing, though not disproportionately laboured, appear desirable to the children and a normal part of everyday life.'

In such a class, reading as a subject does not receive special emphasis, although children are given encouragement and some guidance as and when they show interest in printed or written words. A discussion with such a teacher almost invariably evokes remarks such as, 'Reading is only one of many interests for the children,' or 'We don't push reading; in the right environment it will develop along with the child's other interests.' Implicit in this theory is the conviction that motivation, through interest, is the key factor and that the child will learn to read when he actually feels the need for it. Indeed, the teacher-counsellor often makes it her concern to ensure that the need does arise. At that stage she will be ready to step in and help to guide the child.

There is a marked contrast here between the philosophies of the two types of teachers. The teacher-counsellor who, having arranged what tends to be described as a 'rich environment' is not worried if some children are slow to show an interest in reading. The teacher-leader, who may well provide the same rich school environment as the teacher-counsellor, is generally eager for the children to begin to learn to read as soon as it is practicable. All her beliefs lead her to favour an early beginning rather than a delayed start.

The teacher-leader agrees with the teacher-counsellor that motivation is a powerful factor in the learning situation and that it is likely to develop through interest. But her assessment of reading as a top priority leads her to different interpretations of this belief. First, the teacher-leader does not believe in merely waiting for the child's interest in reading to manifest itself but prefers actively to foster its growth. Secondly, to such a teacher, interest and motivation represent only the starting points. Thirdly, she realizes that motivation is likely to increase alongside mastery of the skill.

Once the child is interested in learning to read, there is a further contrast in the beliefs of the two teachers. The teacher-counsellor sometimes assumes that learning to read will develop naturally, almost as easily as learning to talk appears to do; that exposure to the written word, like exposure to the spoken word, will result in a certain mastery of the skill of reading. In contrast, the teacher who favours planned learning believes that even the strongly motivated child, and more particularly if he is of low intelligence, does not learn to read automatically or incidentally without systematic tuition. The broader the teacher's concept of reading and the greater her ability to analyse the total skill into its component sub-skills, the more comprehensive will be her tuition plans. This teacher may consider learning to read to be hard work, yet at the same time look upon it as an enjoyable and rewarding occupation for both herself and her pupils.

The key to the differences in the beliefs of the two teachers lies in the phrases 'systematically planned learning' and 'incidental learning'. These different views may be summarized as follows. The teacher who favours incidental learning believes that reading is only one of many interests for the young child, that in the right environment a child will eventually want to learn to read and at that point the teacher can help him to do so. Consequently, there is no need for pressure on the child and it is preferable to delay beginning to read until interest and motivation become apparent. In contrast, the teacher who favours systematic tuition believes that learning to read is of prime importance to the child and thus it is to his advantage to learn to read as soon as practicable. To this end, interest and motivation should be actively fostered, and closely followed by a detailed programme of tuition which embraces both systematic teaching and structured learning experiences.

2. Teacher's Different Roles

As might be expected, the contrasting beliefs of these two teachers are likely to result in their adopting contrasting roles in classes working under different organizational procedures. The role of the teacher who favours incidental learning resembles that of the counsellor or consultant, and it is a role which is played in the background rather than the foreground. For much of the day her presence is unobtrusive. Children approach this teacher as they feel the need either to show her what they are doing or to consult her. Meanwhile the teacher herself is closely observing the children and noting when the learning experiences of individual children focus attention on certain points which might be taken up and developed. At these crucial moments, the observant teacher emerges from the background to assume the role of active guide or instructor with one or more children.

The role of the teacher who believes in systematic tuition is more often that of an initiator of events than that of an observer. She accepts that one of her main tasks is to teach children to read and, consequently, one of her important roles is that of a reading instructor. In this role she undertakes direct and systematic instruction, as well as arranging for guided reading practice as part of a predetermined, detailed plan. In consequence, this teacher assumes the role of leader and initiator more frequently than the teacher-counsellor.

Of course, just as the beliefs of these two teachers overlap, so do the roles they play. Teachers supporting either the learning or the teaching theory will adopt, on certain occasions, the role of observer and counsellor and, on other occasions, the role of initiator or instructor. Moreover, even among teachers holding the same belief, the ratio of instruction or guidance in the foreground to observation and consultation in the background varies from teacher to teacher. Nevertheless, for the larger proportion of her time, the teacher-counsellor adopts the role of consultant or guide while the teacher-leader functions in the role of instructor, planner or organizer.

3. Different Classroom Procedures

The basic belief of a teacher about reading, and indeed about primary education in general, not only affects the role she adopts with the children in her class but also the organization and working procedures she favours. Once again it must be stressed that no clear-cut line can be drawn to divide the procedures adopted by the two teachers. In the most extreme cases the observable differences may be startling but in the majority of cases it is more a question of degree.

A teacher who is solely and totally committed to the acceptance of instruction may feel the need to confine children to the classroom and even to desks arranged in orderly rows facing herself and the blackboards. Materials and books to which children have free access may be meagre and opportunities to experiment with paints, clay and other creative materials limited. Reading tuition and practice may be limited to one graded set of readers or charts. Formal instruction may be given to two or three large reading groups. Formality will be the keynote, with children being allowed scant opportunities for informal movement, speech or learning activities. Fortunately, it is now extremely rare to find such a teacher or such a situation.

In most infant classes it is now more usual to find the sort of stimu-lating environment described earlier, in which groups of tables and chairs are so arranged as to leave space to enable children to move about freely. Against such a background informal relationships develop, and work and activities merge in the concentrated absorption of individuals or small groups.

There is a tendency for the teacher-counsellor to favour more infor-mal conditions and procedures than the teacher-leader. Yet it would be just as inaccurate to imagine the teacher-counsellor's class as one in which children do nothing but pursue their individual interests, in an atmosphere of absolute freedom, as to picture the teacher-leader standing permanently in front of rows of children, whose eyes are fixed on her, as she teaches them as a homogeneous unit. In practice, the organization and procedures adopted by the two teachers frequently share so much common ground that a casual visitor to the two classes might not immediately spot the difference in the basic beliefs of the teachers. Both might have the attractive appearance of the modern infant class just described, with children moving freely about, working in groups or individually, and teachers quietly helping. Nevertheless, the similarities noticeable in a superficial glance at the two classes, could disguise important cleavages in purpose and practice, which a closer look at working procedures would reveal.

The differences in the beliefs of the two teachers might first be demonstrated in the timing of the beginning of more formal work in reading. As has already been noted, the teacher-leader is likely actively to encourage an early interest in reading, and she will not hesitate to begin to teach children to read at an early age if she deems them ready; whereas the teacher-counsellor often consciously delays reading tuition. There are dangers inherent in both procedures. The inexperienced teacher-leader may judge a child to be ready to read at too early a stage and so do damage by demanding responses from him which he is too immature to make. The result could well be a spiral of feelings of failure attached to reading. Conversely, the dangers which face the inexperienced teacher-counsellor can lie in a failure to prepare the ground for reading-readiness or to recognize its symptoms when they arise. Thus opportune moments may be missed and beginning to learn to read unnecessarily delayed.

The grouping of children for reading tuition also varies according to the teacher's basic belief. Children working in two or three large reading groups would suggest a teacher who leans towards instruction, while a complete absence of any, even small, reading groups is more likely to indicate a teacher who strongly supports individual learning. Between these two extremes can be found variations in groupings, as well as classes in which children work for part of their time in reading groups and part as individuals. Where there are some permanent or semi-permanent reading groups, the teacher is likely to believe in planned teaching and learning. Sometimes the planning may only take the form of working through a basic reading scheme with the teacher trying to listen to children reading each page and prompting those who stumble over words. Other teachers may have much broader, systematic plans for each group's reading tuition, to include definite teaching and practising of skills rather than the mere reading aloud and prompting technique.

The actual time devoted to reading and supportive activities, as well as the manner in which this time is isolated from or integrated with other activities, can also illustrate the differences in the teachers' beliefs. The teacher who considers reading of prime importance will see that more of the day is devoted to, or slanted towards, reading activities than the teacher who considers learning to read to be only one among many interests. The teacher-leader's belief may result in considerable periods of time being devoted to teacher-directed group reading activities or to the utilization of many of the day's activities to reinforce reading and writing or to both these procedures. In the class of the teacher who favours incidental learning, little or no teacher-directed group work will take place and children may spend a smaller proportion of the day on reading and writing than in the teacher-leader's class.

Yet above all, the factor which most clearly distinguishes the two teachers is the amount of pre-planning of reading activities which they undertake. The teacher who believes in systematic teaching is likely to keep before her, either mentally or in written form, not merely a broad framework of reading development but also a detailed plan of definite stages of progression in the various sub-skills which make up the total skill of reading. Furthermore she will ensure that these stages of learning are introduced systematically in an ordered sequence. The master plan will cover comprehension and interpretative skills, as well as word recognition skills, and the latter will include both the acquisition of a basic sight vocabulary and a knowledge of phonic rules to aid recognition of unknown words. By detailed planning, the teacher will arrange for groups of children or individual children to master the progressively more difficult sub-skills on an ever widening front. This will be done not only in the form of direct instruction but also by the introduction of appropriate games, exercises and books selected either to introduce, reinforce or give additional practice in specific stages of learning. Finally, information regarding the learning which has and has not taken place will be recorded for each child, in some form or other.

The majority of good reading teachers, whether they lean more towards learning or towards teaching, keep some form of records of children's reading progress, even if it is only a note of the page in a basic reader which the child has read aloud to the teacher. The records of the good teacher-leader, however, generally go much further than this. For example, to consider only the word recognition and word attack skills needed in the early stages of reading, actual sight words recognized, single letter and digraph sounds known and phonic rules with which the child is familiar will all be recorded for each individual child. The records may be kept in various forms, by the teacher or the child or by both. The important point is that at any time the teacher is aware of the exact details of each child's knowledge of reading and the next stage he needs to master. The next step in the reading plan does not necessarily have to be included in the child's programme regardless of the activities in which he is currently engaged. The alert teacher will be watching out for opportunities to introduce the work at an appropriate moment; but – and this is one important difference in practice between the teacher-leader and the teacher-counsellor – if an appropriate moment does not arise spontaneously, the teacher who believes in planned instruction will deliberately create a situation in which the next stage of teaching and learning can take place. Clearly, the greater the skill and flexibility of the teacher, the more easily will she be able to adjust her plans to the developing situation.

The teacher-counsellor is also likely to undertake a certain amount of direct teaching followed by further practice, but it is less likely to have been planned in advance for a particular, semi-permanent group of children. The work is more likely to have arisen incidentally with an individual child or with a small transient group of children instead of with an established reading group. In such a situation, it is not easy for the teacher to be certain that appropriate preparatory activities have been carried out by each child and that the necessary reinforcement, practice and review is undertaken in the days which follow.

An example may further clarify this point. Let us suppose that in an informal class in which the teacher believes in incidental learning, during some activity or project a few children become interested in the fact that some words have a silent 'e' at the end. The teacher utilizes this opportunity by trying to develop a generalization about the function of a silent 'e' at the end of a word and its role in altering the sound of a preceding vowel. She may, at that point, have no definite records of which children in this particular group have already met this rule, or are ready for it. Nevertheless, she may try to teach the rule as it applies to one vowel such as the 'a' in 'cake' or to more than one vowel. The brightest child may soon grasp the rule and with a little practice be able to consolidate it so that he can apply it to all the vowels. The slower children would require a great deal of reinforcement, practice and revision in mastering the rule even as applied to one vowel. If such a group of children had comprised a definite reading group, the consolidation of the learning process could have been more easily arranged in the days that followed. But, within the fluid grouping of the informal class, it can prove difficult, if not impossible, to plan for adequate follow up work for every member of an ad hoc group in which the interest in a particular rule first arises. In these circumstances there is a danger that the inexperienced teacher may assume that a rule that has cropped up and been discussed by a temporary group of children has been adequately mastered by all. Thus, even when group teaching does take place in the class of the teacher-counsellor, it may well be less effective than that which takes place in the class of the teacher-leader.

4. Beliefs, Roles and Procedures Influence Choice of Approach

All these factors, the teachers' basic beliefs about reading, the different roles they enact and the varied classroom procedures which result are bound to be deciding factors in the selection of an approach to reading.

In the class of the teacher who favours incidental learning, the early reading vocabulary is likely to spring from the children's own interests and the many school activities in progress. It will be closely linked with speech and writing. Initially children may make their own simple books and later be allowed to choose the published books they wish to read. If books from published reading schemes are used, more than one scheme is probably utilized and the schemes will almost certainly be look-and-say rather than phonic. Teachers who emphasize learning usually show most interest in approaches which advocate or permit the use of a wide range of books and other materials, and they turn away from those approaches in which the materials and suggested techniques are narrowly confined.

The teacher who believes in systematic teaching is more likely to utilize a reading scheme in its entirety than the foregoing teacher. The scheme may be phonically based but need not necessarily be so. Many successful teacher-leaders do use look-and-say schemes, although they tend to employ them somewhat differently from the teacher-counsellors. For instance, they often do more preparatory work, in the form of games, on the recognition of the appropriate sight words before children are introduced to these same words in their books, thus reducing the need to prompt stumbling readers. The teacher-leader who uses a look-and-say scheme will almost certainly introduce some carefully planned phonic training alongside the look-and-say reading and, accordingly, may be interested in published phonic programmes to supplement her look-and-say reading programme.

The ideas contributing to the two contrasting basic beliefs about the acquisition of reading skills, and some of the implications of these beliefs in practice, have been developed in detail because of the importance which is attached to the teacher making this decision as the preliminary step in selecting an approach to reading. It is essential that she decides first whether her own beliefs lead her to emphasize learning or teaching. It is not sufficient to say that in practice she supports both beliefs, for all teachers must necessarily be involved in both processes. It is the degree of emphasis on either incidental learning or systematic tuition including planned teaching and structured learning which is important. Honesty here will prove beneficial because once a firm decision on this point has been taken a foundation will be provided on which the second decision can more easily be taken.

SUGGESTIONS FOR FURTHER READING

A general discussion of learning in school and the teacher's task can be found in chapters 8 and 15 of:

STONES, E. (1967) *An Introduction to Educational Psychology*. London: Methuen.

The results of research in schools in London and descriptions of many situations which illustrate how a teacher can guide the child's learning are given in:

GARDNER, D. E. M. and CASS, J. (1965) *The Role of the Teacher in the Infant and Nursery School*. Oxford: Pergamon.

The importance of systematic instruction is emphasized in:

MOYLE, D. (1968) *The Teaching of Reading*. London: Ward Lock.

GODDARD, N. L. (1969) *Reading in the Modern Infants' School*. London: University of London Press,

shows how the teacher can effectively guide a class of children who are learning to read.

A brief but useful outline of the stages of reading development is given in chapter 2 of:

GATES, A. I. (1935) *The Improvement of Reading*. New York: Macmillan.

5 The second decision — which method and medium?

1. A Dual Decision

Had this book been written ten years ago, the teacher's second decision when considering different approaches to reading would have represented a simple choice between two main methods, phonics and look-and-say. With the introduction of i.t.a. and other new media, the choice of an approach to reading has become more complex. The teacher needs to consider methods and media simultaneously because the published reading materials available are printed in different media utilized according to definite beliefs regarding methods. Accordingly, in this chapter the second decision facing the teacher is considered to consist of a choice of both medium and method.

Broadly speaking, there are still two main categories of method employed for teaching beginning reading and these will be discussed before the details of different media are considered. The reader might find it helpful, at this stage, to confirm the precise meanings of the terms 'medium' and 'method', as they are employed in this book, by re-reading the definitions given in chapter 2 – Terminology.

2. Two Main Methods

A. THE ORIGIN OF THE TWO-METHOD CONTROVERSY

The written form of English does not constitute a perfectly regular representation of the spoken sounds of the language. The relationship between spoken sounds and written or printed symbols includes two types of irregularity. First, certain letters can represent different sounds: for example, the letter 'c' in the words 'cat' and 'cinema' and the letter 'o' in the words 'on', 'rose', 'one' and 'women'. Secondly, certain spoken sounds are represented by different letters or combinations of letters. For instance, the sound 'ee' is written in five different ways in the following words: 'see', 'sea', 'these', 'ceiling' and 'belief'.

Our written language comprises two kinds of words. A proportion of the words follow definite spelling rules, although there are certain exceptions to these rules, while other words are irregular. It is also important to note that many of the most commonly used words fall into the irregular category. For instance, in the list of 'key words' prepared by McNally and Murray (1962), the following irregular words are among those included in the 'thirty basic words accounting for more than one third of the running words met with in ordinary reading, junior or adult': he, the, to, was, all, are, have, one, said.

This mixture of regularly spelt and irregular words has been partially responsible for the contrasting beliefs regarding the advisability of beginning reading by the use of one or other of the main methods. In phonic methods the initial emphasis is on words that follow well-defined rules, while in look-and-say methods the recognition of irregular words or words of different lengths and shapes is encouraged as the preliminary technique. Yet the very nature of written English determines that neither of these methods can function for long in isolation. Supporters of phonic methods have usually found it impossible to avoid the introduction of certain common, irregular words early in the reading programmes. Some authors of look-and-say schemes include a limited amount of phonic work in the later stages of their schemes and, where this is not done, many teachers introduce phonic training alongside the scheme, either by incidental work or by the use of published phonic materials.

B. OLDER PHONIC METHODS

Neither detailed descriptions of phonic and look-and-say methods, nor the history of their development in the teaching of reading would be appropriate in the context of this book, although a few references to sources of such information are given at the end of this chapter. On the other hand, certain aspects of the two methods, and of the educational climates in which they developed and flourished, are closely related to teachers' beliefs, the roles they adopt and the procedures in force in their classes. These particular aspects of the two methods need to be considered as they have important implications for the teacher who is assessing approaches to reading.

Phonic methods began to replace the older alphabetic methods of teaching reading about the middle of the nineteenth century in England and they continued to flourish well into the twentieth century. Certainly the majority of infant schools, even in 1945, were still using phonic reading schemes similar to those originally devised in the nineteenth century, and many continued to do so after that date. It should be remembered that during the nineteenth century and early twentieth century classes were large, the teacher's accepted role was that of instructor, while pupils were expected to sit still, pay attention and work hard. Obedience and industriousness were the qualities teachers most highly prized in their pupils. Rules laid down in the classroom, as well as rules in reading and spelling, were meant to be obeyed. Whether or not children were enjoying themselves or were interested in what they were doing were questions not seriously considered. Reading instruction consisted mainly of teaching the sounds of the letters, combining these sounds into simple words and learning rules which could be applied to more complex words; that is to say, a synthetic phonic method was adopted. The mode of operation was usually oral drill.

It is noticeable that even now, in the minds of certain teachers, this aura of rigidity, discipline, formal instruction and endless drill still clings to the term 'phonics' or 'phonic methods'. Often the teacher who states firmly, 'I don't believe in phonics,' is thinking rather of the atmosphere, working conditions and procedures in force in these older schools, than of what was actually taught in the field of reading and the rationale underlying it. Moreover, such teachers do not always realize that there are different phonic methods.

C. LOOK-AND-SAY METHODS

Look-and-say methods, including both word and sentence methods, did not begin to be widely used in England until the 1940's, although they had been advocated and used by a minority of teachers considerably earlier than this. By 1945 conditions in schools and the whole educational climate had changed considerably from the time when phonic methods of reading were in the ascendency. Classes tended to be smaller and new buildings to be lighter and more spacious. The influence of educators such as Montessorri and Froebel was spreading. In the field of psychology there was considerable support for Gestalt theories, which contributed to the idea of treating whole words or sentences as the basic learning units, a growing emphasis on individual differences and an increased interest in child development.

All these influences contributed to the growth of new ideas in primary education which frequently resulted in changed procedures. The word 'learning' began to replace the word 'teaching' as authoritarian classroom regimes gradually became more democratic. There was a movement towards children learning in small groups or individually rather than being taught in classes or large groups. An emphasis on the interests and happiness of the child began to replace the former concern with discipline and industry. Words such as 'motivation', 'initiative', 'discovery' and 'activity' came to the fore.

New attitudes to primary education in general were accompanied by changes in beliefs about reading tuition. In the more relaxed atmosphere of many infant schools, phonic methods so long associated with authoritarian instruction appeared inappropriate. Look-and-say methods, permitting children's early reading vocabulary to consist of words of high interest value from their own speech vocabulary, regardless of whether these words were regular or not, began to be regarded with more favour. The *Happy Venture Readers* by Schonell and Serjeant, published in 1939, was one of the first look-and-say schemes to gain popularity. It was followed by *Janet and John* in 1949 and *McKee Readers* in 1956, and thereafter by an increasing number of look-and-say schemes. Some of these – for example, *Happy Venture* and one form of *Janet and John* – included lists of phonic words, while others were devoid of phonic training.

Most of the new look-and-say reading schemes to emerge in this sort of educational climate formed a sharp contrast to the old phonic schemes. The reading books were designed to attract the child, motivate him to want to read and interest him once he had begun. The number of books comprising a scheme increased while the size of individual books decreased. These were usually lavishly illustrated and the number of words on each page in the early books was small. The intention was that once the child was motivated to want to read by the attractive appearance of the books, the carefully planned vocabulary control with its slow introduction and frequent repetition of new words, would inevitably lead him on to learn to read easily and happily, individually or in small groups, with a minimum of teacher guidance.

Yet, despite the initial visual appeal of the early look-and-say books and their systematic vocabularly control, teachers soon discovered that, when phonic training was not included in the reading programme, look-and-say as a method on its own failed to provide most children with a tool leading to independent reading. It was frequently not realized that look-and-say schemes required from the teacher as much, and perhaps even more instruction and guidance than the old phonic schemes. With the latter, children had been dependent on the teacher while they learnt the sounds of letters and the simpler phonic rules, but their ability to read independently had increased with their mastery of these rules. With pure look-and-say schemes the time in which children were dependent on their teacher's pacing was extended as they waited to be told the new words introduced on each page. Not only were children unable to utilize phonic clues to help them to decipher the new words but they were often likely to be misled if they attempted to use pictorial clues as a guide to the meaning of the words. In many cases the illustrations were not directly related to the text, being intended as attractive motivating devices rather than as aids to learning.

D. RECENT EMPHASIS ON PHONICS

During the 1950's doubts began to grow regarding the efficacy of look-and-say methods. Teachers in junior and secondary schools expressed concern regarding children who were unable to read being promoted to their schools. Remedial teachers found that failing readers often lacked any knowledge of phonic rules or even of the sounds of letters. Employers complained that there was a decline in the spelling ability of school leavers. Surveys of reading – for example, the Ministry of Education's two pamphlets, *Reading Ability* (1950) and *Standards of Reading 1948–1956* (1957) – revealed disquieting proportions of older school children and adults whose reading abilities were inadequate to meet the demands of a literate society. Much of the blame for this state of affairs was placed upon infant teachers and their use of look-and-say methods.

Accordingly, even at a time when more infant schools were beginning to adopt look-and-say approaches, a movement began towards a return to phonic training, particularly for older, failing readers. The publication of *The Royal Road Readers* by Daniels and Diack in 1954 crystallized the beginning of this movement in England. Subsequently, although details of American publications are usually slow to reach practising teachers in England, news of Flesch's *Why Johnny Can't Read* (1955) did begin to seep through. The publication of British reading materials relating to phonic training continued with *Sounds and Words* (Southgate and Havenhand 1959), *Sound Sense* (Tansley 1961), *Fun with Phonics* (Reis 1962), *A Remedial Reading Method* (Moxon 1962) and *Programmed Reading Kit* (Stott 1962) following in rapid succession. In fact the swing towards phonic work which began as a trickle in the 1950's expanded to a sizeable stream throughout the 1960's, for infants as well as for older pupils. It was augmented by other approaches which, while not designated as phonic, nevertheless emphasized the regularities of our language in the form of systematically planned learning or teaching.

These newer phonic approaches differed from the older ones in a number of ways. Daniels and Diack, for instance, used a different phonic method from the older schemes. They developed an analytic approach to phonics in contrast to the older synthetic approaches. Thus, while synthetic phonic methods had begun by teaching the sounds of individual letters which were combined (or synthesized) to form words, analytic phonic approaches began with whole words which were contrasted with similar words and the differences analysed. Certain of the more recently published linguistic approaches to reading also use this analytic technique of contrasting regular words which differ only by one letter.

Secondly, most of the reading materials relating to the newer phonic approaches show a marked contrast to the materials comprising the older phonic approaches. The latter were usually in the form of basic books, often divided into set lessons, and planned as the sole means of teaching children to read. The newer phonic schemes, on the other hand, are often intended to be used in conjunction with look-and-say reading books. In these cases they may be in the form of small supplementary books of exercises, games and stories or consist entirely of pieces of apparatus and games for children to play, rather than reading books or workbooks. If the new phonic scheme is intended as a total beginning scheme, it almost certainly includes supplementary books, apparatus and games in addition to the basic books.

Thus, many of the newer aproaches to phonics are much better suited to the procedures now prevalent in most primary schools than were the older schemes, planned originally for class instruction. Although they emphasize the regularities of the language and require children to pay attention to details within words, few of them expect the teacher to teach the rules by means of lengthy periods of drill. There is usually as much emphasis on learning as on teaching, with children being provided with opportunities to discover and practise such rules themselves. The newer phonic approaches lend themselves to group work and individual work. They encourage children to be active, both mentally and physically, in the learning process. They can be used effectively in classes working under informal regimes. Yet behind the attractive apparatus of books and the interesting exercises and games carried out in informal conditions, in which the proportion of teacher-instruction to child-learning is small, the majority of these newer phonic approaches represent carefully designed plans of systematic instruction and learning, intended to be put into force regularly and in a specified order.

E. THE COMMON DISADVANTAGE OF BOTH METHODS

Adherents of each of the two main methods, look-and-say and phonics, may consider the two approaches to have little in common. Yet, as far as the child is concerned, the two methods share one major disadvantage. Whether the teacher chooses to begin reading tuition with a look-and-say method or a phonic method, the child is faced with a dilemma because he cannot be given one definite guiding rule to help him to decipher unknown words.

If the child has learnt to read solely by a look-and-say method, without any phonic training, the procedure for learning new words involves merely a choice between consulting the teacher or another child and guessing from the context, which may be lacking in adequate clues. Most teachers, however, use an eclectic approach which mingles look-and-say and phonics in varying combinations. In fact, most authors of phonic schemes generally find it necessary to include, quite early in their texts, certain of the irregular words which McNally and Murray term 'key words'. Thus in the majority of cases the child soon becomes aware that words fall into two distinct categories of regular and irregular, and that when he is trying to read on his own he must tackle these two kinds of words in different ways. It is not intended to imply that the child thinks in these terms. He is more likely to wonder if the unknown word is one which he can 'sound out' or 'build up' or, alternatively, if it is one which he should ask his teacher to tell him. Even if he has not got as far as defining two categories of words, he is likely to be vaguely aware that often when he tries to read a word by either 'sounding' or 'guessing' it, his attempt is wrong. The brighter child frequently learns to juggle with these different techniques reasonably successfully. Other children find the problem confusing and too difficult, and soon develop the habit of just ignoring unknown words.

The child who has acquired some knowledge of phonic rules is certainly in an advantageous position when compared with the child who has received no phonic training; but even he can be misled when he attempts to apply the rules to unknown words. For example, the child who tries to apply the rule 'silent "e" at the end of a word makes o say ō' will find it helpful in deciphering 'bone' and 'strode' but likely to lead him sadly astray when he meets 'done' or 'shone'. In fact Clymer (1963) shows that of forty-five phonic generalizations most commonly taught in elementary schools in the U.S.A., only eighteen are of general utility in that they are applicable to all or a majority of the words the child is likely to meet. For example, the rule 'When a word begins with "wr" the "w" is silent' is a rule having '100 per cent utility' as there are no exceptions whatsoever. In contrast, the rule 'When words end with silent "e", the preceding "a" is long' has only 60 per cent utility: 60 per cent of words, such as the word 'cake', for example, conform to the rule, while 40 per cent, such as 'have', represent exceptions to the rule.

Therefore with a language like English, which includes words which follow certain phonic rules, words which are exceptions to these rules and other words which are quite irregular, all methods, whether they be phonic, look-and-say or eclectic, suffer from one major disadvantage: the child cannot be presented with a single mode of attack on unknown words. It is not easy for literate, book-loving adults, most of whom learnt to read quite easily, always to appreciate the drawbacks of this situation. We just do not know how much this difficulty delays children's reading progress, but practical experience with children beginning to read and with failing readers suggests that it presents a formidable stumbling block to many children, and in particular to less able children, often discouraging them from attempting to read or write new words.

3. A Choice of Media

A. ALTERNATIVES TO t.o.

For more than a century, certain educators who believed that the inconsistencies of our spelling system represented a serious stumbling block to children's attempts to learn to read advocated and experimented with various ways of overcoming this difficulty. Using the definition suggested earlier, that 'medium' is the term employed for the actual form of written or printed symbols used to represent the spoken language, the various media proposed as suitable for beginning reading may be divided into three broad groups.

In the first place, there is traditional orthography (t.o.); that is, the ordinary English spelling system using a twenty-six-letter alphabet – the medium by which we learnt to read and write and the medium in which most adult publications are printed.

The proposed alternatives to t.o. as media for beginning reading may be divided into two groups, described as 'signalling systems' and 'simplified spelling systems'. In the signalling systems, the twenty-six-letter alphabet and the traditional rules of English spelling have been accepted, but various signals have been superimposed on many of the letters to form alternative media for beginning reading. These signals have sometimes taken the form of letters and digraphs printed in different colours according to the sounds they represent. In other systems various marks have been printed or hand-written on or near certain letters: for example, an oblique stroke through a silent letter or a curved line under two letters which form one sound. Such marks are usually termed diacritical marks. In both the colour codes and the diacritical marking systems, these marks usually act as signals to the correct pronunciation of the words, although in certain cases they merely represent danger signals, warning the child that letters do not sound as they might have been expected to do. In all signalling systems, the signals are only intended to be used in the early stages of learning to read, after which they are expected to be discarded.

Within the group of media classified as simplified spelling systems can be found alterations and additions to the twenty-six-letter alphabet, as well as amendments to spelling rules. The various alterations are all proposed with a view to regularizing and simplifying traditional spelling, the aim generally being to achieve a one-to-one correspondence between spoken sound (phoneme) and written symbol (grapheme) – or as near an approximation to this ideal as is practicable.

The development of alternative media to t.o. for the early stages of reading tuition has important implications for the teacher in her choice of an approach to beginning reading. The fact that published reading materials in alternative media are now available in Britain means that teachers are offered the opportunity of by-passing the one great disadvantage common to phonic, look-and-say and eclectic methods used with t.o. For the child, the dilemma of how to attempt to read an unknown word can be banished, or at any rate diminished, with the introduction of a regular code as the initial reading medium.

I. i.t.a.

As an alternative to t.o., the medium with which teachers are most familiar and the one in which most reading materials are available is the

Initial Teaching Alphabet (i.t.a.) devized by Sir James Pitman and first used in England in 1961. It represents one example of a simplified spelling system, using a forty-four-letter alphabet of which twenty-four letters are the same as in the traditional alphabet. The main spelling rule employed is a one-to-one correspondence between spoken sound and written character. Absolute regularity has not been aimed at as, with an eye to easing the transition to t.o., certain examples of a character representing more than one sound and of a sound being represented by more than one character are retained. i.t.a. is one of the approaches to beginning reading which is examined in detail in chapter 10.

2.   OTHER AVAILABLE MEDIA

Although many other media for beginning reading have been proposed by innovators and tried out by experimenters, few have been utilized in published materials which are readily available for purchase by teachers in Britain at the present time (1969). However, a number of examples of media in the category of 'signalling systems', and all employing colour codes, are currently published in Great Britain. Gattegno's (1962) *Words In Colour* and Jones' (1967) *Colour Story Reading* are probably the best known, but the Bleasdales' (1967) *Reading by Rainbow* represents a further example of the use of coloured letters in published reading materials. *Words In Colour* and *Colour Story Reading* are fully discussed in chapter 10.

Published reading materials utilizing systems of diacritical marks are not currently available in this country but this fact does not necessarily preclude teachers from using such media. A teacher who becomes convinced of the value of employing a signalling system which superimposes differentiating marks on t.o. can have suitable reading materials duplicated or can arrange for ordinary t.o. reading books to be marked in the appropriate manner. (One of the authors has vivid memories of watching an infant teacher, some twenty years ago, spending her lunch times marking copies of *Radiant Way* with what she called 'fairy marks'. Her system was similar to some of the 'new' systems of diacritical marks now being advocated.) Teachers who may be interested in experimenting with diacritical marks will find a sample of Fry's Diacritical Marking System on the opposite page.

*A Sample of Prose in Fry's Diacritical Marking System**

"Traditionally one of the first tasks of the infant school was to teach children to read. It is still, quite rightly, a major preoccupation, since reading is a key to much of the learning that will come later and to the possibility of independent study. In many infant schools, reading and writing are treated as extensions of spoken language. Those children who have not had the opportunity at home to grasp the part that they play are introduced to them by the everyday events and environment of the classroom. Messages to go home, letters to sick children, labels to ensure that materials and tools are returned to their proper place; all call for reading and writing."

---

* The above extract, marked according to Professor Fry's system, is from the Plowden Report: *Children and their Primary Schools*, Vol. I, para, 583, H.M.S.O. 1967.

B. ADVANTAGES AND DISADVANTAGES OF REGULARIZED MEDIA

Teachers might find it helpful if the most important advantages and disadvantages of using some form of regularized medium for beginning reading tuition, in preference to t.o., are summarized at this point.

I. ADVANTAGES

a. A regularized medium, whether it takes the form of a signalling system or a simplified spelling system, appears to make the earliest stages of learning to read easier for the child.

b. If the medium represents a complete code to pronunciation, the child can learn to adopt one invariable technique for attempting to decipher new words, and the employment of this technique is almost certain to guarantee success.

c. The use of simplified regularized media, in place of t.o., is thus likely to lead to a number of beneficial effects for the child, including the following:

    i. there is less likelihood of failure;

    ii. he soon experiences success, pleasure and satisfaction;

    iii. his desire to read and his interest in reading increases;

    iv. he more quickly becomes independent of the teacher.

d. The task of helping children to learn to read becomes less arduous for the teacher, with the result that she has more time to devote to other aspects of the curriculum and the special needs of individual children.

e. When the medium represents a simplification and regularization of the writing system,* children's ability to express themselves freely in writing will be facilitated and their free written work will be likely to increase in quantity and quality. Attempts at spelling words in the regular medium are likely to be more often correct than when t.o. is the medium.

---

* Colour codes and diacritical marking systems, for example, while they may help to simplify reading do not automatically help children with their free writing, as various forms of spelling for one sound still exist. A complete regularization of the writing system would provide for each sound being represented by only one form of written symbol. i.t.a., for instance, while not an absolutely regular writing system, approaches very much nearer to this standard than does t.o.

2.   DISADVANTAGES

a.   Certain difficulties may be encountered by both the children and their parents when the medium of instruction differs greatly from the traditional spelling system in use outside school. The closer the appearance of the new medium to t.o. the less important is this difficulty likely to be. This may suggest that, on this count, signalling systems may have an advantage over simplified spelling systems which employ numerous new characters.

b.   The quantity and variety of reading materials published in new media is often limited.

c.   The published reading materials may be restricted to one scheme of books or apparatus, applicable only to a definite method and with certain procedures which the teacher does not support. This disadvantage applies particularly to signalling systems.

d.   Children who have to move to another school before they have transferred from the alternative medium to t.o. are likely to experience difficulty.

4. The Linked Choice of Medium and Method

It is clear that in the teacher's second decision the choices of medium and method for beginning reading are closely interrelated, and also that the decision regarding them partially represents an interpretation of the teacher's basic belief about reading. A few examples of how the first two suggested decisions might work out in practice may help to illuminate the relationships between the various factors discussed so far.

The teacher-counsellor, as she stresses learning rather than teaching, is likely to encourage children's individual work springing from their interests and activities. This attitude must necessarily preclude from consideration those new media which are represented by a limited range of published materials designed to be utilized in formal teaching situations. Certain colour codes, for example, fall into this category. The obvious choice of medium for this teacher lies between t.o., with its wealth of reading materials, and i.t.a. with its expanding list of publications. Both these media lend themselves to the use of either a look-and-say or a phonic method, although the teacher-counsellor is likely to favour look-and-say. If this same teacher also strongly favours the simultaneous development of reading and writing, and especially when children's early free writing is a spontaneous off-shoot of the activities going on in the school, she is bound to be attracted by a simplified spelling system such as i.t.a. which has demonstrated its potential in this field. A third medium also presents a possible choice for the teacher-counsellor and that is some system of diacritical marking. This teacher is often the very one who prefers the child to have hand-made reading materials, such as picture books with his own words or sentences as captions, and so on in the earliest stages. In these circumstances, a lack of materials printed in the medium might not be considered a drawback.

The teacher-leader who believes in planned teaching and learning rarely favours a look-and-say method used with the medium of t.o., unless she also intends to introduce some phonic training at an early stage alongside it in the reading programme. She cannot fail to examine hopefully all new phonic schemes, whether formally or informally orientated, and whether they are planned as basic schemes or supplementary schemes intended to support a look-and-say approach. If this teacher also believes in activity, informality and individual work, her interest in phonic materials will be restricted to those which allow her beliefs to be put into practice and she will avoid phonic approaches which demand formal teacher instruction. In addition, this teacher with her emphasis on systematic learning is bound to look with both interest and sympathy at any new system designed to bring simplicity and regularity to the medium used for beginning reading.

There is little doubt that many teachers will experience difficulty in making the second decision, as numerous permutations of basic beliefs with different combinations of preferred medium and method are possible. Nevertheless, the teacher may take comfort from the thought that once she has taken the first two suggested decisions, her task of assessing reading approaches will appear much less perplexing. Certain approaches will be automatically eliminated as a result of the decisions, while others may be easily discarded by a brief examination of the reading materials relating to them.

SUGGESTIONS FOR FURTHER READING

Everyone interested in the controversy about look-and-say and phonic methods should read the following book, in which Professor Jeanne Chall of Harvard University, analyses sixty-seven research studies comparing different approaches to beginning reading:

CHALL, J. S. (1967) *Learning to Read: The Great Debate*. New York: McGraw-Hill.

Further details of the various methods and their historical development can be found in:

DIACK, H. (1965) *In Spite of the Alphabet*. London: Chatto & Windus. and

FRIES, C. C. (1962) *Linguistics and Reading*, chapter 1. New York: Holt, Rinehart & Winston.

A clear description of an eclectic approach to reading, beginning with a look-and-say method (an approach which was used by many teachers from the 1940's to the 1960's), is given in:

SCHONELL, F. J. (1942) *Backwardness in the Basic Subjects*, chapter 7. Edinburgh: Oliver & Boyd.

A brief statement on the phonic word method, which is a recent development in phonic methods, can be found in:

DANIELS, J. C. (1966) 'The place of phonics.' In DOWNING, J. A. (ed.) *The First International Reading Symposium, Oxford 1964*. London: Cassell.

Suggestions for further reading about *i.t.a.*, *Words in Colour* and *Colour Story Reading* are listed at the end of chapter 10, in which these three approaches are discussed in detail. Readers who are interested in a much earlier attempt to use colour in order to differentiate between the various parts of a word should refer to:

DALE, N. (1899) *On the Teaching of English Reading*. London: Philip, and to *The Dale Readers* which accompany this book.

Fry's system of diacritical marks is described fairly fully in the first of the following four articles, while the remaining three articles discuss the results obtained in one of the U.S. Office of Education's First Grade Reading Studies:

FRY, E. B. (1967a) 'The diacritical marking system and a preliminary comparison with i.t.a.' In DOWNING, J. A. and BROWN, A. L. (eds.) *The Second International Reading Symposium*, pp. 156–168. London: Cassell.

FRY, E. B. (1966) 'First grade reading instruction using diacritical marking system, initial teaching alphabet and basal reading system.' *The Reading Teacher*, Vol. 19, No. 8, pp. 666–669. Newark, Delaware: International Reading Association.

FRY, E. B. (1967b) 'First grade reading instruction using diacritical marking system, initial teaching alphabet and basal reading system – extended to second grade.' *The Reading Teacher*, Vol. 20, No. 8, pp. 687–693. Newark, Delaware: International Reading Association.

FRY, E. B. (1967c) 'Comparison of beginning reading with i.t.a., d.m.s. and t.o. after three years.' *The Reading Teacher*, Vol. 22, No. 4, pp. 357–362. Newark, Delaware: International Reading Association.

6 The third decision — which reading materials?

1. The Teacher's Choice

The teacher's search for the best way of helping children to learn to read continues indefinitely as new approaches, new media, new reading schemes, supplementary materials, games and apparatus are devized, published, reviewed and advocated. The teacher reads about these new ideas, listens to lectures and whenever possible examines the materials. She compares them with the approaches she is currently using.

While engaged in these assessments, the teacher's mind is likely to be crowded with a kaleidoscope of ideas reflecting all the factors which have bearing on the choice. She pictures the children in her class and the situation in which the learning will take place. She is probably aware of whether her own emphasis rests on the difficulties of the task itself or on the individual difference in children, the ways in which they learn and their all-round development. The teacher may recognize, closely related to this emphasis, her basic beliefs about reading as being slanted towards either incidental learning or systematic tuition, and her own preferred role and procedures. She may also have reached conclusions regarding medium and method. Reflections on this multiplicity of relevant factors may have led the teacher to formulate a large group of criteria against which possible approaches to reading need to be measured.

No approach is likely to satisfy all the criteria, if only because certain of them are either conflicting or mutually exclusive. It is thus clear that what every teacher, and particularly every head teacher, needs to do is first to place the criteria in order of priority and then to select the approach which most nearly fulfils the top priorities in her list. Making the first two decisions suggested in this book, regarding her own basic beliefs and her preference for a particular medium and method, should have taken the teacher a long way towards sorting out her own ideas regarding the priorities.

A few teachers and other educators may well take exception to the general theme of this book because more attention seems to be paid to the teacher's beliefs and preferences than to the interests and needs of individual children. Certainly the differences between children in such characteristics as intelligence, linguistic ability, interests and motivation are important and should be taken into account when selecting reading approaches. Yet to speak of every child being unique, as no doubt he is, does not necessarily mean that each child requires a different approach to reading, although the Plowden Report (1967) certainly implies the need for individually selected approaches when it states '. . . the most successful infant teachers . . . choose methods and books to fit the age, interest and ability of individual pupils', and 'Instead of relying on one reading scheme, many teachers use a range of schemes with different characteristics, selecting carefully for each child.'

The idea that a teacher should personally select a reading approach for each individual child in her class probably goes far beyond what is necessary, is certainly at variance with current practices, and, moreover, represents an impractical proposition for most schools. An awareness of individual differences should not blind us to the fact that in most classes there are large groups of children with common attributes and needs. Even if children's needs were placed at the top of the list of priorities, the conclusion might still be drawn that the majority of children in a particular class would be likely to benefit from a common approach to reading, while other approaches might prove beneficial for a minority of children. Acceptance of such a conclusion would suggest that the concept of an individual approach to reading for every child is unnecessary.

The facts regarding the use of reading schemes in infant schools might be taken to indicate that most teachers accept a theory of the existence of common needs in the majority of the children in a class. Goodacre (1967), for example, found that out of 100 infant schools and infant departments in her London investigation, seventy-nine used one basic reading scheme, fourteen used two schemes and three used three schemes, while only four schools used no basic reading scheme at all. These figures suggest that in ninety-three per cent of infant classes teachers consider one or two basic reading schemes adequate to meet the needs of most children.

While one would hope for more flexibility and variations in approaches than Goodacre's survey indicates to be the case, it could, nevertheless, prove dangerous to press too far the ideal of selecting reading schemes carefully for each child, unless a staff of stable and experienced teachers is available. To do so with inexperienced or changing staff could result in a medley of reading materials being picked up and discarded by individual children under the banner of 'freedom of choice' or 'catering for individual differences'. In such circumstances only a few of the brighter children would be likely to 'pick up' reading. There is no doubt that an able and experienced teacher, even with a class of forty children, can go a long way towards catering for children's individual needs. In contrast, it is probable that the inexperienced or temporary teacher will find it easier, and that the children will make more progress, if the needs of many children are seen as group needs and if the reading schemes available are limited to a small number.

The authors are inclined to believe that a teacher's personal preference for a particular reading approach may be equally as important or more important than the individual differences between children. A teacher will only be able to do her best work, accompanied by optimum benefits to the children, if the main approach to reading in her class is one in which she believes and which lends itself to the procedures which she prefers. Certain teachers, for example, may feel uneasy about working in the informal atmospheres of some infant schools. It may be that their characters, personalities, beliefs about reading, or habits have led them to prefer more formal procedures. Whatever the reason, such a teacher will not be happy with an approach to reading which demands an informal classroom régime. Conversely, the teacher whose beliefs are centred on incidental learning would never willingly choose a reading approach which was clearly designed for a somewhat authoritarian teacher-pupil relationship.

Yet the selection of a reading approach which calls for the ordering of new reading materials is not something which can be undertaken frequently. A newly appointed member of staff is indeed fortunate if she is given this choice. More often the majority of the required reading materials are already there, having been selected by the head teacher. It is thus usually the head teacher's main responsibility to assess and select reading approaches. The wise head teacher will undoubtedly do this in relation to the beliefs of the staff as a whole, and she will then also try to allow new members of staff a measure of flexibility to adopt an approach which at least leans towards their own beliefs and preferred procedures. Such flexibility will be more easily achieved if two or three basic schemes are available in a school rather than only one. There is also the possibility that discussions between teachers and encouragement from a head teacher may persuade a new teacher to try an approach about which she has misgivings, and that the doubts may thereby be dispelled.

The circumstances in schools are such that it is doubtful if the teacher who is trying to arrange the criteria for assessing reading approaches in order of priority will ever find it possible to actually place each individual child's needs at the top of the list. To do so would entail assessing the background and needs of every child and then providing him with a teacher with the appropriate beliefs and attitudes, working with the right materials in the ideal environment. The actual situation is quite the contrary. The teachers are the most important part of the school environment: they are there when the child enters this environment. The twin tasks of first recognizing children's needs and, secondly, catering for them through the selection of an appropriate reading approach can only be undertaken through the operation of the beliefs, attitudes, abilities and aptitudes of the particular staff, in this particular situation.

It is because of the foregoing reasons that throughout this book, although the differences between individual children are by no means discounted, there is an emphasis on the beliefs and preferences of teachers

2. The Reading Materials

The head teacher or class teacher engaged in appraising approaches to reading, having defined her basic beliefs, preferred roles and procedures, made decisions regarding medium and method, and arrived at an order of priorities among the many possible criteria of assessment, is finally ready to give serious consideration to the third decision, namely, which specific approach? At this stage, a careful examination is required, not only of the reading materials themselves, but also of articles, reviews, publishers' blurb and teachers' manuals relating to the approach. It is suggested that this examination might be made as listed under the following headings.

A. THE AUTHOR

I. A TEACHER'S MANUAL

The first line of enquiry should be to ascertain whether the author of the reading scheme, the inventor of the game or apparatus or the originator of the approach has written a teacher's manual, pamphlet or article setting out the rationale underlying the approach and explaining how the reading materials are intended to be used. If so, the first step should be to read what the author has written. If no such material is available, one is entitled to question the reason. Is it because the author is uncertain about his own aims or is it that he has not given sufficient thought to intended methods of procedure and so is not in a position to express his ideas clearly in writing? Alternatively, is the idea itself and the form which the reading materials have taken so familiar to every teacher that neither aims nor procedures need be suggested? If so, one may ask what is new about this approach? Does it merit serious consideration?

2. THE AUTHOR'S BASIC BELIEFS

Next the teacher needs to consider the basic beliefs of the author about reading. Is the author's main emphasis on reading as a skill which requires systematic teaching or on the child as an individual who will learn to read incidentally as part of his general development? Are the teacher's own beliefs about reading in line with the author's? If not, has the author anything to offer the teacher? If the author's views on reading tuition are diametrically opposed to the teacher's, it is unlikely that either the teacher or the children in her class will find satisfaction in using the scheme.

On the other hand, when an author's main ideas do not exactly coincide with her own, the teacher need not summarily reject the approach. To have clarified one's own philosophy about learning to read should not necessarily lead to the assumption that a different philosophy has nothing to commend it. Reading an author's description of a new approach can sometimes illuminate some aspect of learning to read about which one has been vaguely uneasy without the doubts having actually been crystallized. To find someone precisely formulating an idea of which one was only half conscious can represent a stimulating experience, likely to initiate a fresh line of development in one's own thinking. Thus, while it is important for a teacher to formulate her own ideas, it is equally important to keep an open mind so that other views are not rejected out of hand.

3. AUTHOR'S ASSUMPTION REGARDING TEACHER'S ROLE AND PROCEDURES

Implied roles and suggested procedures for any approach are closely related to the author's general views about reading. Accordingly, the teacher must consider which role the author assumes the teacher will adopt, as well as all the details of procedure implied in the author's suggestions or instructions for utilizing the reading materials. It is not uncommon for a reading approach to be condemned by a teacher who has used it in a totally inappropriate situation, as in the glaring example cited here.

A certain infant teacher, working under extremely formal procedures began to use the *Pilot Reading Scheme* (Davenport 1953). She soon reported that the children were not succeeding because the vocabulary load of the first four books was too heavy. The vocabulary load of these four books was twenty-seven, thirty-two, forty-five and seventy-seven words respectively and there was little overlap of words between books. If these four books were to be used as a graded series of reading books from which a teacher would instruct children in the skill of reading, the vocabulary load was certainly too heavy, but such a procedure was far from the intention of the author.

Miss Davenport, the author, states clearly in her teacher's manual, 'In this scheme experience comes before reading.' She had assumed that in an infant class children would be engaged in many activities and that there would be a great deal of discussion regarding the activities. Accordingly, she devised four pre-readers about a toyshop, a kitchen, a farm and a post office: books which were pre-eminently picture books designed to attract and interest the child. She proposes that as well as classroom centres of activity round the four themes, children should be taken to visit such places. It is only after all this activity and discussion relating to one of these centres of interest that the author suggests placing the appropriate picture book in the book corner. There children will pick it up and enjoy examining the colourful pictures. Later the teacher may read the sentences to a few children while they look at the pictures. Finally, certain children will begin to try to read for themselves the sentences containing words which are by now so familiar to them in the spoken form. In such a setting, the vocabulary of these four books takes on an entirely different aspect. Many children will soon master these words and be able to progress to the main reading books in the scheme and to the supporting picture dictionaries and attractive supplementary story books.

The teacher in the formal classroom should not have blamed the reading scheme for the children's failure: the blame was hers for not selecting a scheme suited to her own beliefs and procedures. Had she first read what the author had written about the scheme, she would have appreciated that the author's beliefs and aims were in direct opposition to her own and, moreover, realized that her own class, with children sitting in rows of desks awaiting reading instruction, represented an entirely different environment from that envisaged by the author.

4. AUTHOR'S BACKGROUND AND EXPERIENCE

A teacher engaged in the appraisal of a new reading approach would also be well-advised to pay some attention to the author's background and experience. For example, it is prudent to consider whether the author had experience as a teacher and, if so, with what age of children and whether they were normal children, retarded children or children in special schools. An author with teaching experience is likely to devise a reading approach which is particularly appropriate to the kind of children whom he or she has taught. An infant teacher is often able to produce a good infant reading scheme and a remedial teacher a scheme designed to overcome the difficulties experienced by older retarded readers. It does not follow that the scheme could not be used effectively with different children in another age group. It does mean, however, that a teacher considering a new approach which was intended for children unlike those in her class or group should ask herself if the scheme has been tried out successfully with a group of children resembling hers. If such experiments with diverse groups of children have been undertaken, the teacher can be assured that this fact will be mentioned in the teacher's manual or publisher's blurb.

Occasionally, proponents of new approaches to reading have little or no teaching experience. It would be unfortunate if their proposals were ignored merely on this score, as a problem is sometimes more clearly perceived by someone standing slightly apart than by the person actually engaged in the day-to-day working situation. The interested outsider, knowledgeable in a related field of study may, by a flash of insight, clearly illuminate a problem which has bewildered the practitioner. For example, an educational psychologist, a linguist, a member of the medical profession, a lecturer or a professional writer may well have something valuable to contribute to reading teaching. An educational psychologist may be able to apply his general knowledge of children's learning to the specific process of learning to read. A linguist, with his interest in the structure of the language, may throw light on the nature of the task to be mastered.

In such circumstances the teacher needs to consider whether the specialist in a related field is concerned with a particular aspect of the subject of reading which she herself believes to be important. If this is so, the teacher needs to know whether the originator of the scheme worked in close collaboration with teachers during the formative stages of the development of the idea, or if the approach has been successfully used with children similar to those in her class. Alternatively, she may decide that the case put forward by the author is sufficiently strong to merit trial with her own group of children.

5. OTHER EDUCATIONISTS' VIEWS ON THE AUTHOR'S IDEAS

Finally, the teacher would find it helpful to know what other people think about the author and his ideas. Such information goes beyond that usually found in teachers' manuals or publishers' advertisements and blurb, which sometimes include letters from satisfied customers, as such letters can only have been included because they throw a favourable light on the approach. Reviews and critiques may give some help, but one needs to be sure that the critic is not himself author or supporter of a rival reading approach. General articles on reading which mention the approach in teachers' journals are likely to be more helpful. Most useful of all are written reports or lectures by teachers who have used the approach and can describe how it works in practice.

The foregoing lines of enquiry regarding the author of a reading approach, his ideas and experience, should precede a close examination of the materials intended for the children's use. In this way the vital factor of the rationale underlying the approach can be appreciated before attention is focused on less important details such as attractive illustrations.

B. THE MEDIUM AND METHOD EMPLOYED

The second step in examining the materials comprising a reading approach is much simpler than the first step referring to the author. The teacher merely needs to ascertain that the medium employed is the one on which she has already decided and that the main method for beginning reading tuition is her preferred one of either look-and-say or phonic. If the scheme is look-and-say, she will also want to note whether it begins with sentences or with discrete words, whether phonics are introduced or not, and if so at what stage and in what quantity. If it is a phonic scheme the teacher will need to determine whether an analytic or synthetic phonic approach is employed. It is not anticipated that a teacher will alter her opinions on either medium or method at this stage of the examination of the actual reading materials. Such decisions will have been taken well in advance. Reading the teacher's manual will have supplied the straight answers to these two questions; an examination of the children's books or equipment will simply supply a few additional details.

C. CHILDREN FOR WHOM THE MATERIALS
ARE APPROPRIATE

Three related questions should be asked referring to the children for whom the reading materials were originally devised and the children with whom the teacher considers using them. For exactly which children were the reading materials originally planned? Do the children with whom the teacher is considering using the materials resemble the original group of children fairly closely? If not, are the materials likely to prove perfectly suitable for the proposed group of children?

I.   CHILDREN FOR WHOM MATERIALS WERE PLANNED

The advertised description of a new approach frequently gives the impression that it would prove suitable for use with a wide range of children, including those of different age groups, levels of intelligence, home backgrounds, and interests, as well as children following a normal pattern of reading progress and others who have already failed. It would be exceptional for an approach to prove equally effective with all these varied groups of children. It is also rare for an author to produce a scheme actually intended to cater for such a wide range of children, although it is sometimes found that the market is wider than at first anticipated by the author.

Authors of successful reading schemes or pieces of apparatus have usually devised them with a particular group of children in mind. The teacher appraising reading approaches would probably find it enlightening, when examining the teacher's manual and pupils' materials of a new scheme, to imagine what an exceptionally honest piece of blurb might have said regarding the children for whom the approach was planned. Examples of such descriptions might run as follows:

1.   'This scheme was devised for use with infants of average intelligence coming from middle class homes in the suburbs of a town.'
2.   'These books were planned for educationally sub-normal children of about eight who have poor spoken vocabularies and a limited range of interests, and who have virtually not begun to learn to read.'
3.   'This approach to reading is intended specifically for seriously retarded readers, mainly boys, in secondary schools in deprived areas, who have acquired a small sight vocabulary of words but whose reading ages are well below seven.'

Obviously, a teacher must rely upon her own critical judgement of the scheme, but discussions between teachers at conferences and courses would help her to come to a more balanced decision on this point.

2. CHILDREN IN THE CURRENT GROUP

To define the general characteristics of the children in the school, class or group for which the reading approach is being considered is the simplest part of the problem facing the teacher. Even when allowance is made for individual differences between children, there are nevertheless general characteristics which any group of children can be said to possess. The average levels of age, intelligence, home background and interest are the important factors here. Most teachers will not find this assessment difficult. The main danger is that their genuine interest in the children with whom they are concerned may cause them to be optimistic when estimating average levels. It is not uncommon to find a head teacher describing the average level of intelligence of children in the school or the socio-economic level of the parents as 'about average' when both are considerably below average. It is because teachers regard them as 'such nice children' and 'such co-operative parents' that they occasionally tend to be optimistic about average ratings. But objective appraisal of general characteristics of the relevant group of children will facilitate the selection of appropriate materials.

A teacher's knowledge of the area from which the school or institution draws its pupils must clearly affect her choice of reading materials. Here we are not thinking so much of the fact that children from contrasting socio-economic levels show considerable differences in average levels of intelligence, linguistic competence, desire to read and readiness for reading tuition but rather of their general backgrounds and interests. A primary-school teacher working in a deprived area, for instance, would probably find the interest level of a reading scheme such as Taylor and Ingleby's (1960) Let's Learn to Read appropriate for her pupils, as it was planned for city children in a poor area. She might equally well select Berg's (1969) Nippers, consisting of stories with working-class, town backgrounds. A remedial teacher working with older children in the same area might choose the Inner Ring Books, (Pullen and Rapstoff 1967), in which the stories concern adolescents living in a city area in which many houses are being demolished. In contrast, a teacher in a primary school in a high socio-economic area in the suburbs may feel that the middle-class background of the children portrayed in such schemes as *The McKee Readers* (McKee 1956), *Key Words Reading Scheme* (Murray 1964), *Queensway Reading* (Brearley and Neilson 1964) and *Ready to Read* (Simpson 1966), with their cars, lawns, picnics and seaside holidays would appeal to her pupils.

The increasing number of coloured children to be found in schools in certain areas represents an additional facet of children's backgrounds and interests. Their teacher may think that such children would appreciate books in which both coloured and white children are included in the illustrations and stories. Certain reading schemes published in the U.S.A. are now making a point of this. No reading scheme intended for children in Britain has yet done so, although the series of supplementary books entitled *First Words* (Southgate 1968a) does include pictures of coloured and white children playing together.

Teachers will find it simpler to make the assessment of the other important factor of whether the children are following the normal pattern of developmental stages of reading progress or whether they can be described as retarded or backward children who have failed to make normal progress. This assessment is less likely to be subjective than the preceding one.

3. GENERAL APPLICABILITY OF MATERIALS

Although the teacher's first line of search will be primarily directed towards finding a reading approach originally devised for pupils who closely resemble her own, a perfect match between the teacher's own group and the children for whom the reading materials were planned can hardly be expected. Minor deviations in the characteristics of the two groups of children may be unimportant. In certain instances the teacher may be able to adapt or supplement the materials by way of compensation.

Problems arise, however, if the pupils the teacher has in mind as she considers the materials differ widely from the pupils whom the author had in mind. In these circumstances, serious thought needs to be given to

'What shall we say?'

'Try to say it.'

the advisability and the practicability of attempting to use these particular materials. Certain people might question the wisdom of a remedial teacher who is seriously considering using infant reading materials with older juniors or pupils in secondary schools, and equally the judgement of the infant teacher who is examining materials designed for older retarded children. Yet it can sometimes happen that a set of reading materials embodies certain features, such as interest, content, illustrations, methods of approach or modes of operation which the teacher considers particularly apposite for the group in question – features which she has failed to discover in other materials which at first glance may appear more appropriate.

For example, the *Griffin Readers* (McCullagh 1959) were originally written for older retarded pupils, but the strong interest appeal of pirates may attract a boy in an infant class who has previously shown little desire to read and may thus motivate him to want to learn. In contrast, *The Mac and Tosh Readers* (Ashley 1938), which were intended for infants, may appeal to an older retarded pupil who is interested in animals, primarily because the stories concern two dogs but also because they are devoid of pictures of young children which would make the books appear childish.

In these circumstances, the question of the adaptability of the materials must be examined. The teacher's manual may discuss how the materials and the suggested procedures could be adapted in different circumstances. There may also be accounts, either in the manual or in articles in teachers' journals and other books on reading, of the materials having been used with pupils who differed in certain characteristics from the original ones. A teacher reading accounts of such experiments can judge for herself the extent of their success. But more often than not, any judgement regarding the adaptibility of the materials must rest on the teacher's previous experience of the interests and reactions of children similar to her current class or group.

D. OPTIMUM SITUATIONS

The situation in which children will be learning to read must clearly influence the teacher in her selection of an approach. Broadly speaking, the optimum situation in which to use any set of reading materials is one closely resembling the one which the author had in mind when the scheme was devised. Among the relevant features of a situation in which learning to read is to take place – and excluding those features already discussed such as the teacher and the children concerned – may be included the type of educational institution itself and the area in which it is situated, the actual physical conditions, the other children who form part of the group or class and the educational 'climate' of the institution.

I. THE EDUCATIONAL INSTITUTION

The type of educational institution in which the reading approach is to be used clearly represents an important factor affecting the choice. Infant, primary, secondary and special schools differ from each other and from such institutions as remedial centres, child guidance clinics and hospital schools, not only in the pupils for whom they cater, but also in their size, physical conditions, internal organization and staff, as well as their aims. Although the variations possible in this particular factor are self-evident, one or two examples may serve to illustrate their different requirements from reading approaches.

In infant classes, where incidental teaching and learning may be in operation almost throughout the day, it is much easier to integrate reading with speech, drama, written work, story-telling and creative work than in upper primary classes or secondary schools, where more rigid time-tabling is in force, or where teachers are specialists in particular subjects rather than all-round practitioners. Reading materials for the latter classes thus need to be more or less self-contained, because reading skills more likely have to be acquired from the actual textbooks (and practised by use of the supporting workbooks and supplementary materials) in set time-table periods. It is also often of advantage for reading schemes chosen for older pupils to be so designed that the inherent plan of progression can easily be grasped by the teacher who is not a reading specialist, because many teachers of older pupils who find themselves called upon to teach reading know very much less about the subject than their colleagues in infant classes.

Reading materials selected for use with remedial groups or individual retarded readers in child guidance clinics and remedial services also require additional emphasis on certain features in order to meet the special requirements of failing pupils: for example, especially attractive and interesting materials which differ as much as possible from those used in normal classes, built-in success mechanisms and fun in the form of games in the place of work from books.

2. THE PHYSICAL AMENITIES

The physical conditions in which the reading tuition is undertaken may determine the choice of an approach. For instance, small classrooms, so crammed with dual desks that the only available floor space is narrow aisles between columns of desks, can still be found in certain primary schools. Moreover, if the classes are streamed according to ability, it is more than likely that, as Morris (1966) discovered, the slowest stream which includes the most backward readers will be allocated the least suitable accommodation. A teacher who finds herself in such a situation must necessarily avoid reading materials whose use demands a good deal of physical activity on the part of the children. A reading scheme such as Gertrude Keir's (1947) *Adventures in Reading* and *Adventures in Writing*, with its large selection of carefully graded basic books, workbooks and supplementary stories would be one possible practical choice for the teacher of backward juniors in such circumstances.

Peripatetic remedial teachers visiting schools to help groups of retarded readers frequently find themselves working in unsuitable conditions. Small medical rooms, staff-rooms and even cloakrooms have, on occasions, all been used for such work. Sometimes not only are blackboards, bookshelves and cupboards for storage lacking but even tables of suitable size and height. Such a situation would preclude the use of a valuable reading scheme for backward older pupils, such as Miles (1951) *Active Reading*, as it requires desks or tables on which children can spread out large workbooks and play card games.

In contrast, many modern infant classrooms have not only book corners, painting corners, dressing-up corners and the like, but also space in which children can move about. The physical conditions in such rooms provide opportunities for group reading, individual reading tuition, games and activities connected with reading and writing, creative work arising from reading, speech and drama. In short, they are suited to all kinds of informal approaches to reading but are unsuitable for class teaching and formal approaches to reading.

3. OTHER CHILDREN IN THE GROUP

When the children for whom the teacher is selecting a reading approach constitute part of a larger group such as a class, another factor exists which must necessarily limit the choice. For example, many approaches to reading are more appropriate when all or most of the children in a class are in the early stages of learning to read than they would be for a group of non-readers who form part of a class in which the majority can read. Approaches incorporating singing games and all noisy activities or activities involving much physical movement, work best when most of the class can be swept along on the same tide of interest and enthusiasm. It can prove a little more difficult to get the best out of such a scheme with a vertically-grouped class of infants, and virtually impossible to do so in upper primary or secondary classes, where the majority of children are working at a more advanced level of quiet, formal work.

In fact, the older the children in the majority group and the higher their reading attainments, the more difficult it is to choose appropriate reading approaches for a small group of non-readers or slow readers. Not only are noisy activities unfeasible because they will disturb other children, and activities requiring space debarred through lack of space, but the feelings of the non-reader require special consideration. Activities in which he would happily participate if the class consisted entirely of older non-readers like himself would embarrass him if they were introduced before his contemporaries who were fluent readers. In a remedial group in a separate room the retarded older pupil might enjoy stories, games with flash cards, simple card games, puppetry, and drama and creative activities as part of reading tuition. In his own class he would be likely to prefer books and workbooks which, at least from their external appearance, do not differentiate him too much from his friends.

4. THE 'CLIMATE' OF THE GROUP

The situation in which the reading tuition will be undertaken comprises more than the physical conditions such as space, fitments and equipment, and the people who work within the physical conditions, such as teacher, tuition group and other children. Every school, class or group has a distinctive 'educational climate' which experienced visitors to schools can quickly spot. It is made up of the beliefs of the head teacher and the staff, and the manner in which these beliefs are put into practice through the social relationships existing between the staff themselves, between teachers and children and between the children themselves. It demonstrates itself in the arrangements of the physical phenomena within the building, in the roles adopted by the teachers and pupils and in all other aspects of procedure.

The teacher examining a particular set of reading materials needs to assess the 'climate' of the situation in which they were intended to be used. If this 'climate' differs widely from the 'climate' of her own school, class or group she would be wise to forego this approach and search for one more in keeping with the climate in her own situation. One singularly inappropriate choice of reading scheme (*The Pilot Reading Scheme*) in relation to the climate of a particular class and school has already been discussed in detail on page 58. Other examples would be the use of *The Gay Way Series* (Boyce 1959) in a school which believes in a look-and-say approach or the use of *The Happy Venture Readers* (Schonell and Serjeant 1939) with upper juniors or secondary school pupils.

E. THE SCOPE OF THE MATERIALS

I. COMPLETE SCHEME OR SUPPLEMENTARY MATERIALS?

A cursory examination of a set of children's reading books or apparatus will rarely suffice to show either the exact scope of the scheme or the gradient of difficulties within it. If the teacher is not to be disappointed and if the children are not to be faced with a frustrating task, the teacher needs to allow herself sufficient time to look very carefully into this point.

First, it is necessary to establish whether the scheme is intended as a complete reading scheme or as supplementary materials. This decision is not always as simple as it appears. Of course, it depends on what one means by 'complete'. It is unusual, in Britain, for any scheme to be considered so entirely complete that children's reading experiences could be confined only to the materials in the scheme without recourse at least to class-library books. In contrast, many American schemes have such a wealth of supporting materials in the form of work-books, exercises, supplementary stories, phonic training, card games and record charts that in this sense they are more nearly 'complete' than most British schemes. On the other hand many British teachers, even if they were offered such extensive reading schemes, might refuse them on the grounds that they would dislike working within such a clearly defined framework, with little need or opportunity to venture beyond the materials provided.

Yet the opportunity to select a reading scheme which represents a mere skeletal framework and so provides the teacher with freedom to introduce supportive reading activities on her own initiative, demands that the teacher should be precisely aware of the scope of the scheme and its limitations. Viewed from the angle of supporting materials, the less the teacher is going to be dependent on a basic reading scheme, the more it becomes essential that her knowledge of supplementary reading materials should be not only wide but also technically competent regarding grading of difficulties. This is particularly true for the teacher who dispenses altogether with a basic reading scheme. Surrounding children with a wealth of interesting, attractive books does not absolve the teacher from competence in one of the technical skills of her profession, that is the ability to grade books according to reading difficulty by analysing the content and gradient of their vocabulary, their sentence structure and the complexity of the ideas they contain.

2.   LEVELS AND GRADIENTS OF DIFFICULTY

Whether the reading materials constitute a basic reading scheme or supplementary materials, the teacher needs to be certain of the range of attainments which they cover and the gradient of progression between the beginning and final levels of difficulty. Both the outer limits and the inner stages require appraisal. A teacher's manual in the case of a reading scheme, and a descriptive paragraph or two in the case of supplementary materials, should provide guide lines on this point. In addition, a detailed examination of the materials themselves is also essential for accurate assessment.

When appraising a reading scheme the teacher will want to know exactly where the scheme begins and ends. Is it meant for complete beginners or does it assume that children already know a few words or sounds? To discover this it is vital to examine more than just the first page or two of the pupil's book. Many schemes look deceptively simple if one only glances at the early pages which may have only one or two words or a single sentence on them. Yet, by turning even a few pages or looking at the middle and end of the first book, it can be realized that no beginning reader could have progressed so far in so few pages. Schemes devised for retarded older pupils are particularly prone to be misleading in this way. Any scheme intended for pupils who have barely begun to read, which within the space of one or two small books appears to bring them to levels of attainment equivalent to reading ages of six and a half or seven, should be submitted to an extremely thorough scrutiny.

The upper attainment levels of infant reading schemes show great variations and not all teachers are sufficiently aware of this fact. The following table shows the approximate number of words introduced in certain well-known look–and–say schemes.

Table 1. Vocabulary Content of Look-and-Say Schemes

READING SCHEME	NUMBER OF BASIC BOOKS	APPROX. TOTAL OF WORDS INTRODUCED
Key Words (i) for infants	18	487
(ii) extended to older pupils	24	880
Happy Venture	10	1164
Queensway	26	1178
Janet and John (Whole-word course)	7	1201
Time for Reading	30 (sections)	1715

Additional details regarding the vocabulary of these schemes are given in the Appendix. These tables illustrate not only the contrasting levels of attainment on completion of different schemes but also the dangers of attempting to establish common levels between books in the various schemes.

The teacher who relies fairly heavily on a reading scheme may be particularly interested in those schemes which reach the highest levels of attainment, and may favour a scheme which will take the children into the stages commonly reached in junior classes. *Happy Venture* which leads on to *The Wide Range Readers* (Schonell and Flowerdew 1953), and *Janet and John* leading on to *High on a Hill, Days in the Sun* and *The Five-and-a-Half Club* (O'Donnell and Munro 1956) represent two examples of such extended schemes. In contrast, a teacher who relies only slightly on a reading scheme, because she prefers to supplement it by much incidental reading and to move children off quickly on to a wide range of other materials, may well look favourably on a shorter introductory reading scheme such as *Key Words Reading Scheme* (Murray 1964).

Not only reading schemes but supplementary stories, phonic books, apparatus and games also need assessing with regard to scope and gradient. Sets of supplementary readers for example can be all at one level, can have a number of books at different levels of increasing difficulty or can incorporate a progression from one book to the next throughout a series.

3.   SUPPLEMENTARY TO WHAT?

When the reading materials do not form part of a reading scheme, special attention needs to be given to the question of what they are expected to supplement, as well as the precise stages at which they are intended to support the basic tuition. The teacher needs to consider whether the reading programme in her class will be strengthened by the addition of these particular story books or games. Some of the more recently published supplementary story books appear so attractive that they will clearly have great visual appeal for children. Accordingly, the teacher needs to be on her guard lest the attraction of subject matter, presentation and illustrations lures her into the acquisition of materials which are not the most appropriate for the stages of learning reached by her pupils. If the vocabulary of the stories selected is rather easy for the children concerned, no great harm is done. If the books are too difficult – and this is more often the case – the teacher may unwittingly be encouraging children to skip over the reading matter and use the books simply as picture books.

A wide variety of supplementary books at the very earliest stages although chosen to stimulate the child and inspire him to want to read, can to some extent hinder his progress. For example, a child who is able to read the first book of a look-and-say scheme which has a vocabulary load of say thirty-five words may be unable to recognize more than a few words outside this total. Yet, if a number of small story books supplement this basic book by employing the thirty-five words he knows, together with a few new words of high interest value, and having strong contextual clues, this same child will be able to read them almost on his own. This will not only prove a satisfactory experience for him but will reinforce his earlier learning and so prepare him for the next book in the series, which may only introduce another twenty or thirty new words, embedded in a large body of familiar words. In contrast, the child who, after reading his first basic book, tries to read other supplementary books – even at an extremely simple level – may encounter thirty to forty words in each story, of which at least half may be new words. At a conservative estimate, such an experience might expose him to over 100 new words. The further the child progresses in reading, of course, and the wider his reading vocabulary becomes, the greater will be the range of supplementary stories which he will be capable of reading on his own.

The teacher choosing supplementary story books needs to bear in mind not only the vocabulary but also the subject matter and interest levels of the basic books which they are expected to supplement. If the reading scheme is restricted to the everyday happenings of a normal family, the supplementary stories required to enliven and enrich this diet may be folk tales, adventure stories, tales of imagination or humour. If the basic books lean towards girls' or boys' interests, the teacher will want to redress the balance in the subject matter of the supplementary stories. Accordingly, supplementary story books for children using a look-and-say scheme need to be scanned carefully to ensure that they will actually support the reading programme. In this respect, the vocabulary overlap between them and the basic scheme, the total volume of new words to be mastered and the story content all represent important features.

Teachers using look-and-say approaches to reading will frequently feel the need for some form of supplementary phonic materials, in addition to supplementary story books. The teacher who has analysed the content and structure of the materials already in use in her class and viewed it against the broad framework of what needs to be learnt, will be in a strong position for formulating exactly what is needed in the way of supplementary phonic training. The required materials may take the form of workbooks, as for instance, *Six Phonic Workbooks* (Grassam 1959) or exercises included in a series of children's books, as for example, *Let's Learn to Read* (Taylor and Ingleby 1960), *The Royal Road Readers* (Daniels and Diack 1957), *Sounds and Words* (Southgate and Havenhand 1959) or *Step up and Read* (Jones 1965). Alternatively, the selected phonic training may consist of games which children can play in pairs or in groups, as in *Programmed Reading Kit* (Stott 1962) or *Fun with Phonics* (Reis 1962).

Teachers who prefer to begin reading with a phonic approach may have greater problems in selecting supplementary materials for the earliest stages than teachers using look-and-say approaches. Reading apparatus, either isolated sets or parts taken from another phonic scheme, may be found which truly supplements the chosen phonic scheme, but finding appropriate supplementary stories is not so easy. The child whose reading diet has consisted of regular words of similar composition and length may badly need exciting stories which will stir his imagination. Yet such stories must necessarily contain many irregular words which will not respond to the application of the simple phonic rules with which the beginner is familiar.

There are two reasonable possibilities for the teacher here, and it may be that a combination of the two will prove the only possible solution to finding supplementary stories for the phonic beginner. First, certain phonic approaches do have small supplementary story books in which the majority of words are regular, while common look-and-say words are included; for example, the supplementary story books accompanying *The Royal Road Readers* and *Sounds and Words* represent examples of such stories. Their own prescribed selection of regular words inevitably proves a limiting factor as far as story content and flow of style is concerned, although within these limits certain of the stories manage to be reasonably interesting for the beginning reader.

The second possibility is to choose supplementary books in which the vocabulary content is small but there is constant repetition of words and phrases so that even a child who is phonically-orientated will have a chance of mastering the irregular words on a look-and-say basis. *Read It Yourself Books* (Melser 1960), *This is the Way I Go* (Taylor and Ingleby 1965), *Mouse Books* (Piers 1966) and *Methuen Caption Books* (Randall and McDonald 1968) are examples of the simplest of such supplementary books. They can be followed by real story books containing frequently repeated phrases such as certain of the traditional tales: for example, *Chicken Licken* and *The Three Little Pigs*. Just as with look-and-say beginners, so with phonic beginners, the further the children progress the greater the possible range of supplementary stories from which to make an appropriate selection.

One further point should be made regarding the selection of appropriate supplementary reading materials of all kinds. Such materials should not be regarded solely as filling the gaps in the teacher's main reading programme. Even when supplementary materials cover exactly the same ground as is already being covered by the teacher in her own way, there is value in books or apparatus which provide the child with the opportunity of practising newly acquired skills in a different and interesting fashion. Children's learning is more likely to be reinforced without boredom if both look-and-say words and phonic rules are practised in as many different ways and varying contexts as can be devised.

F. STRUCTURAL AND FUNCTIONAL COMPETENCE

The teacher selecting reading materials of any kind needs to assess the author's competence in carrying out the task he has set himself. Both structural and functional competence are involved; the two aspects being related rather than opposed to each other. Structural competence depends mainly on the author's knowledge of theories of learning and of language structure, and is clearly demonstrated in the construction of the materials. Functional competence relates to whether the materials will actually work, if used as suggested, with the appropriate children. Competence in both aspects is something which teachers will not find too difficult to assess, and the greater their experience of teaching reading, the more accurate will be their judgements. How often one hears the experienced teacher express the view that there is too great a difference in the difficulty levels of Book 2 and Book 3 in a certain look-and-say scheme or that the author of a phonic scheme in which two phonic rules are introduced on one page cannot have much practical experience of teaching reading!

In look-and-say materials, structural competence will be judged partially on the words selected, the gradient of their introduction and the adequacy of arrangements for their repetition in a variety of situations which, while avoiding boredom, will ensure that learning takes place. Another point which needs to be considered is whether the text develops a story in such a way that the child can use the contextual flow in order to interpret the meaning of unfamiliar words. Many early reading books are deficient in this respect, as they consist of strings of words and phrases which do not tell a story but are merely abbreviations of a story which may exist in the author's mind. In the sphere of structural competence the teacher will also need to examine the sentence structures used by the author with a view to deciding whether they will assist or impede the child's reading. An obvious example of unsuitable sentence structure for early reading books is the habit of breaking up a sentence of reported speech by the insertion of a phrase such as 'said the boy'. For example, in the sentence, 'Give me my coat,' said the boy in a loud voice, 'or I shall go home and tell my mother,' the insertion in the middle of the sentence can interrupt the young child's grasp of the content of the actual speech.

In phonic schemes and apparatus, the problems of structural competence are somewhat, although not entirely, similar. An easy gradient of the introduction of new sounds and rules needs to be planned, but, with phonic materials, the repetition essential for adequate learning is further handicapped by the limitations imposed by a restricted vocabulary of regular words. Structural competence may be judged very largely by how the author overcomes this problem and also by his ingenuity in devising different and interesting ways, not only of practising known skills, but also of transferring the training received to unknown words.

Functional competence usually depends on the author's experience of the practical teaching-learning situation. His own teaching experience or acquaintance with practising teachers, his experience and observations of children and his first-hand knowledge of school conditions and procedures are all important background factors influencing the construction of the materials so that they prove functional or otherwise. The author deficient in practical classroom experience could well produce logically structured materials, unable to be faulted on this score, but which would not work because they represented an adult manner of learning, because they had no appeal for children or for many other reasons. One could imagine, for instance, that a linguist, unacquainted with modern schools and having little experience of children, could produce reading materials which were structurally sound but not functionally competent. For example, certain teachers who might admire the structural competence of Fries's (1966) *Merrill Linguistic Readers*, may yet doubt the functional competence of this scheme for use in British infant schools. The teacher can best judge the functional competence of any reading materials by asking herself 'Will this work with the children in my particular group? Are the words, stories and interests suitable for the children? Will the pupils want to do, and be able to do, the exercises suggested? Can they follow the rules for the games? Do children of this age like books of this size and activities of this kind?'

G. PRODUCTION

The manner in which the publisher has produced the reading materials can either complement or impair the structural competence displayed by the author. Yet the best reading materials for any particular purpose are not necessarily the most expensive and most lavishly produced; rather is it a question of appropriateness. Little research has been undertaken on such features as the size and shape of books, the size of print, the amount of print on a page and the manner in which it is spaced out, the value of conformity or variety in presentation and so on, in relation to different ages. Neither is much information available on the effects of different types of illustrations in children's books, although Vernon (1962) does point out that children do not find it as easy to interpret pictures as many adults imagine they do. Accordingly, in appraising many of the features relating to the production of reading materials, teachers will find themselves relying mainly on their own common sense, experience with children and aesthetic standards.

Two conclusions regarding the production of children's books have, however, become commonly accepted. The first is that younger children and those in the early stages of reading should have books containing relatively small amounts of reading matter and, secondly, that the smaller the hands, the smaller the size of book which can be easily handled. In contrast, with pieces of apparatus, the child of five or six often does not possess the manipulative skill necessary for handling tiny pieces of card. Yet shape as well as size of book needs considering. For instance, a supplementary story book which is 8 inches (200 mm) wide and 5 inches 125 mm) deep is not nearly as acceptable to infants as if these two dimensions were reversed. The child cannot easily support such a wide book if he is sitting on a chair in a book corner, and if he is sitting at a table the opened book takes up so much width that the child requires the space of a dual table.

Furthermore, the common practice of displaying supplementary books on open book racks in infant classes emphasizes the importance of certain features of the covers. The wide book takes up twice as much shelf space on the open book rack as the taller, narrower book. The covers of books meant for display on book racks should be stiff and, if they are intended for beginning readers, it is preferable for them to have pictures relating to the contents shown on the covers. Both this picture and the title should dominate the top half of the cover which is visible above the wire or rod used to hold the book in position. Books with dust jackets require special consideration. Pleasing jackets may disguise dull bindings unlikely to attract children. Moreover, the dust jackets will soon be torn, unless the teacher does a good deal of advance preparation to make them serviceable.

Basic reading books, which are frequently bought in graded sets of six or more and stored away in piles in cupboards, pose a different problem relating to covers. If children are to be responsible for distributing and collecting these books, each grade in the series requires some distinguishing feature other than merely the title of Book 1 or Book 2 on the cover; for example, the colours of the bindings or the cover pictures should be different.

Both reading books and reading equipment of all kinds must be sufficiently sturdy to withstand rather rough handling. Bindings which come apart, pages which tear easily and card which is not strong enough for its purpose are unsatisfactory from both the teacher's and the child's point of view.

The spacing and positioning of print also requires consideration. There are still certain publications for beginning readers in which half a word is printed at the end of one line of print and the remainder of the word at the beginning of the next line of print. Such a procedure merely constitutes an additional complication to the child who is in the early stages of learning to read. Long paragraphs should be avoided for the beginner because he finds it difficult to keep his place. On the other hand, the practices of projecting, rather than indenting the first word in a paragraph, and also of phrasing stories so that each line of print represents a meaningful unit, seem of definite help in the early stages of reading.

In certain books, one finds new stories beginning half way down a page. In these circumstances, young children do not always appreciate that a new story has begun. Children are also inclined to miss the odd phrase or sentence in a passage of prose when it is inserted over a picture at the top of a page or under a picture at the foot of the page. In fact, it is possible that uniformity of presentation rather than variety may help children in the earliest stages by both illustrations and blocks of print being arranged in identical positions on succeeding pages. There is one particular sort of page sometimes found at the beginning of introductory reading books, consisting of small illustrations labelled with the appropriate nouns, which can prove misleading unless a uniform procedure is adopted. In certain instances, some words are underneath while others are at the side or above the illustrations. It would be preferable for all the words to be positioned uniformly in relation to the pictures, and it is probable that demarcation lines between illustrations might prove even more helpful.

Whether the illustrations found in reading materials are considered good or poor is a matter of subjective judgement on the part of individual teachers, and in many instances opinions are bound to differ. Nevertheless, illustrations which are either incompetent or ambiguous – for instance, those in which children have the faces of adults or in which it is difficult to distinguish between a sheep and a dog – should not be accepted. The teacher also needs to be clear about the function of illustrations, particularly in early reading books. In certain books, for example, *Oxford Colour Reading Books* (Carver and Stowasser 1963), the illustrations have a teaching function in that they help children to recognize the related words. In other schemes, for example *Key Words Reading Scheme* (Murray 1964), the illustrations are extraneous to the text; their function is seen as one of attracting the child to the book rather than of depicting the meaning of the words or sentences adjacent to them.

A teacher's assessment of the standard of production of any reading materials should be closely related to their purpose and to the author's competence in devising them. Appropriateness in materials, print, illustrations and general presentation is the most important attribute to look for.

H. EXCELLENCE

There are certain authors with good ideas who are accomplished at devising structurally and functionally competent reading materials. There are likewise publishers skilled in the production of reading books and apparatus of high quality or of particular appropriateness. An ideal marriage between author and publisher, however, is not always arranged. The first-class author, particularly if he is not yet well known, may not be fortunate enough to have his work accepted by a first-rate publisher. On the other hand, even the good publisher does not always judge correctly when accepting manuscripts and the result may be a work of mediocrity disguised by the trappings of high quality publishing. Yet, when the highest levels of authorship and publishing are amalgamated, the results are reading materials of real merit or even of excellence.

In this context, the following are relevant questions which might be considered. Has the author gone beyond the bounds of competency in devising something which is original, imaginative, absolutely appropriate, inspirational or of high literary merit? Has this special flair of the author's been supported by high publishing standards, in the production of appropriate materials, whether these be simple, sturdy pieces of apparatus or beautiful books with sensitive or exciting illustrations? If so, the result will be reading materials of excellence rather than of mediocrity and these are what the teacher with foresight is seeking.

I.   SPECIAL FEATURES OF READING APPARATUS

Many of the points already raised regarding the selection of suitable reading materials apply equally as well to apparatus as to books. There

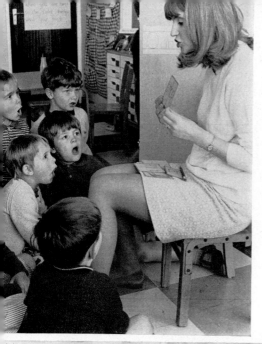

'Say it with me.'

The variety
of a reading period

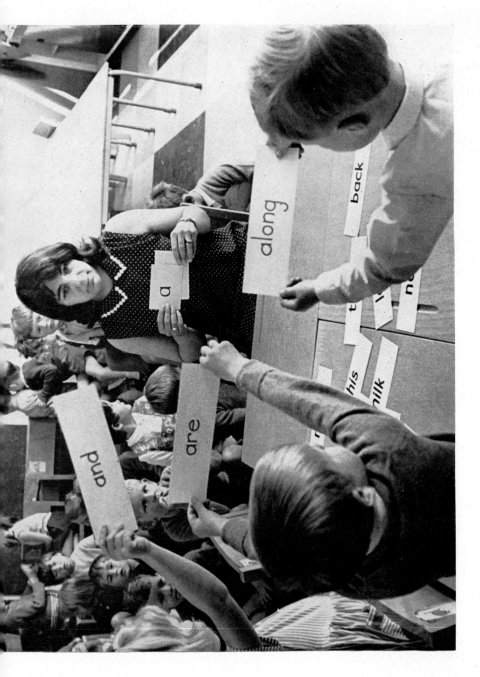

'Words beginning with . . .'

are, however, several additional features requiring special consideration in the choice of reading equipment, apparatus and games. The following points require particular attention.

I.   THE PURPOSE OF THE APPARATUS

A close examination of certain equipment and games, ostensibly described as 'reading apparatus', will reveal that they are unlikely to further children's reading progress, particularly if children are expected to use them on their own. The only purpose of such apparatus would appear to be that of occupying children while the teacher is busy with something else, and even this object would rarely be achieved. Yet it is quite possible for apparatus which 'occupies' children happily also to serve the function of helping them learn to read.

Thus the first and most important question to ask about reading apparatus is, 'What is its purpose?' We need to know precisely how its use will further the child's reading progress. For instance, the game may be designed actually to teach something by guiding the child to make certain correct associations, such as between words and corresponding pictures. This function of games and apparatus, however, is rare, unless the teacher is expected to take a major role when the game is being played. More often the apparatus is intended to reinforce what has already been taught, to give additional practice in some newly acquired skill or to test the child's knowledge of something partially or imperfectly known. In the latter case, the game should have some built-in mechanism whereby the child can recognize and remedy the incorrect responses.

An example of that familiar type of activity of matching words printed on small cards to their corresponding pictures may serve to illustrate the different purposes such an occupation can fulfil. Let us suppose there are six cards, 2 inches (50 mm) square, each with a picture on the front – for example, a dog, a cat, a girl, a boy, a flower, and a house – and six small cards, 2 inches by half an inch (50 × 15 mm), each with one of these words printed on it. If the child is meant to match words to pictures on his own, it is difficult to accept that any useful purpose will be served. The child either knows the words or he does not. In either case he will have completed the activity in a minute or less. He will not know whether he is right or wrong until the teacher has time to come and check. This is a typical example of the time-wasting, valueless use of some items of reading apparatus now on the market. On the other hand, if the teacher uses these cards with a group of children, instant correction of errors could occur together with reinforcement of correct responses, so that the children would be helped to learn the words.

Now suppose that the pieces of card have certain matching devices on the front. These may be different colours, background patterns or jig-saw edges, meant as clues to guide the child towards correct matching. The teacher may believe that the child is being guided to learn that this particular written symbol, 'dog', is said as 'dog' and means the animal in the picture with which it is matched. But is this what the child is learning? More often than not he will pay attention only to the minimum clue likely to lead to the correct result: yellow card matches yellow card or a 'sticking-out' bit here fits into a 'going-in' bit there. The printed word 'dog' and its association with the picture of the dog may be far from his thoughts. Clues on the front of apparatus, however, although they may help to ensure that correct matching takes place, should be considered as guidance rather than as true self-checking devices. With such apparatus, when the teacher can be certain, without having to make constant checks, that correct matches between pictures and words have been made, the learning should be reinforced by some additional activity. For instance, the child may draw the picture in his own book and write the word besides it.

The same type of apparatus for matching words with pictures can also be designed for more advanced stages of learning. The original straight-sided cards, for example, may include the relevant word printed on the back of each picture card. If both square and oblong cards are placed word-side-up on a table, the child can match pairs of words, one on a square card with one on a small oblong card. This can be mere matching of visual shapes without the words being known, but if the square cards are then turned over to expose the pictures, the child is being taught what the words say. Yet he may have matched the first sides wrongly! Therefore, a self-checking device must be included, such as identical pictures on the reverse sides of the oblong cards.

The set of apparatus just mentioned can be used at a later stage in learning by the child who knows most of the words. In this case the cards act as a test, reinforcing the learning which has already taken place and pointing the way to mastery of the unknown words. In this instance the square cards are placed with pictures facing upwards. The oblong word cards are matched to the pictures. The child then turns over the picture cards, exposing the words on their reverse side. If he is correct, identical pairs of words will be exposed. If a few words are wrong, the child would need to have been trained to re-learn them from the cards, then to re-shuffle the cards and begin again, until all are correct.

This one example has demonstrated how similar sets of apparatus can serve different purposes or no useful purpose at all, depending on whether self-checking devices are employed, what these devices are and where they are placed, and also on how the teacher trains the child to use the apparatus. It also serves to illustrate how carefully teachers need to examine reading games and apparatus, in order to decide the exact purposes for which they were designed and the precise stage in the learning process at which they may profitably be utilized.

2. THE PLACE OF APPARATUS IN THE READING PROGRAMME

Reading apparatus and games forming part of a reading scheme will usually be described in the teacher's manual, and will relate to definite stages of development within a composite plan of reading tuition. In these circumstances, it is comparatively simple for the teacher to decide whether the apparatus in question will form a valuable supplement to her own reading programme. The reverse is true when discrete games and sets of apparatus are under consideration. The difficulty of selection is increased if the teacher has no master-plan for her own reading tuition, and it is certainly a problem which defies solution if the teacher has not first analysed the purpose of each game and allocated it to a definite developmental level. It is when such assessments have not been made that children can be observed picking up and discarding odd sets of reading apparatus as random and quite valueless occupations. Accordingly, the teacher choosing an assortment of reading apparatus needs to consider in detail whether each particular game can enrich what she is already doing, or whether the relevant teaching and learning could be more profitably undertaken in some other way.

Odd reading games wisely chosen could serve two main functions. First, they may help to fill in gaps in the teacher's basic programme. Secondly, by presenting a novel way of learning, they can motivate children and offer them variety while providing additional practice in certain items which have been superficially learnt. The teacher using a phonic approach, for instance, might find games which encourage speedy recognition of common, irregular words to be a useful adjunct to the reading programme. In contrast, a teacher using a look-and-say approach, and wishing to supplement it by some phonic work, would probably prefer the play approach of games and apparatus favoured by Stott (1962) and Reis (1962) rather than the more formal techniques associated with the introduction of phonic charts and written exercises. Of course, if the main reading programme revolves round a well-organized set of apparatus it could well be that story books, work cards or written exercises would provide a more acceptable addition to the class stock of reading materials than would further apparatus.

3. THE SERVICEABILITY AND ORGANIZATION OF APPARATUS

Games and apparatus consisting of numerous small pieces of card can so easily constitute an irritating and recurring problem for both teacher and children. The pieces become lost or damaged, the game is spoiled and the teacher has to spend time in replacing or renovating. Even more seriously, certain sets of apparatus require so much of the teacher's time on advance preparation before they can first be utilized (for example, in cutting up card, varnishing it, preparing containers, labelling and so on), and so long to distribute and collect every time they are used, that the few minutes the children actually spend on using them make a mockery of the whole procedure.

The teacher choosing reading games and apparatus might first consider the appropriateness of the size of the pieces the children are meant to handle. The pieces must also be durable, not easily broken, bent, torn or disfigured. They should generally be made of wood or very strong card with a glossy finish which will repel dirt.

Secondly, any set of apparatus comprising many pieces requires a sturdy and appropriate container; an envelope or packet rarely proving adequate. Certain seemingly sturdy cardboard boxes with loose lids can be deceptive. It is so easy for the lid to be knocked on to the floor, stood on, and the edges broken. It is a pity that more containers with fixed lids, or even strong bags with drawstrings at the necks, are not produced by manufacturers. If the container is a box it should be of such a size and shape that the pieces will easily fit into it, and in an obvious fashion, so that even young children can undertake this task.

Thirdly, both the containers and the individual pieces of apparatus should be clearly labelled and carry identification marks. This is particularly important when a series of identical boxes hold cards of identical size and shape. Young children may not be able to read or understand descriptive labels intended for the teacher's information, such as 'Vowel Digraphs' or 'Irregular Word Dominoes', yet even the youngest are capable of placing all the cards with red backs in the red box and those with blue backs in the blue box, or the cards which have a number 5 in the corner in the box which has 5 on the lid, and so on. Furthermore, manufacturers of such materials do not always appear to realize that two children who are sitting at the same table may be using two different sets of apparatus in the same series. If individual pieces, similar in size and shape, carry no special identification marks, they can just as easily become mixed during play as at the clearing away stage.

4. INSTRUCTIONS FOR USING APPARATUS

Instructions for using the apparatus or for playing the game – both the instructions intended for the teacher and those for the child – should be clear and unambiguous. It is not sufficient to assume that all teachers know exactly how the equipment should be used nor that they will all interpret ill-defined instructions in the same manner. One of the authors once observed a piece of equipment being used by three teachers in three quite different ways. Each teacher confessed that she had found difficulty in understanding the instructions for using this gadget. It later turned out that not one of the observed modes of operation represented the one the inventor had in mind! Moreover, it would have proved a much more useful piece of equipment if the inventor's instructions had been clearly phrased so that teachers used it as was intended.

Instructions for the use of equipment which children are to use individually or for group games need to be brief, simple and appropriate to the age of the pupils and to the levels of their reading ability. Complicated procedures or rules inevitably lead to misuse of apparatus or quarrels in games. If it is going to take the teacher a long time to instruct children in the techniques of using the apparatus, she should consider whether this time is justified in view of the learning which is likely to take place. Often this is not so. On the other hand, it can be profitable to initiate children into certain techniques and rules capable of being employed again and again with similar materials at more advanced stages of learning. Mastering the rules of the game of 'Bingo' or learning to use certain simple pieces of equipment designed for programmed learning, are examples of such techniques which, because of their wide applicability, merit time being spent on their mastery.

5. SELF-CHECKING DEVICES

When the purpose of reading apparatus was discussed earlier, some mention was made of self-checking devices. It is such an important point that it cannot be overstressed. A situation in which children should have to wait for the teacher to come and check what they have done, before they can proceed to another activity, is inexcusable. Yet many sets of published apparatus do not have built-in systems of self-checking. The teacher needs to be quick to spot this flaw. Sometimes she may decide that certain equipment, lacking in self-checking devices, has so much to offer in other respects that it would be worth purchasing it and adding self-checking devices herself. More frequently the equipment is not worth the extra work involved.

Self-checking devices which may be found on published equipment, or which the teacher may add, include the following: pictures, numbers or patterns on the back, check-cards or reference lists which can be consulted after the game or task is completed, clues visible to the opponent or partner but not to the child actively engaged, battery-operated equipment which flashes different coloured lights when a response is correct or incorrect and stencils or templates which pinpoint errors. It should also be remembered that a clue such as a jigsaw shape, or a special **colour** or design on the upward-facing side of equipment, should not be rated as a self-checking device. These simple clues merely act as a guide to correct responses and they are only of value in the earliest stages of learning a particular process. Such clues should be withdrawn as soon as possible, and true checks placed in such positions that they cannot be consulted until after the activity is completed.

J.   THE COST OF READING MATERIALS

Head teachers who are assessing reading materials of every kind cannot avoid considering their cost. Yet a fair appraisal of actual cost must take into account many more features than merely the prices quoted in a catalogue. Without having examined the purpose of the materials, their scope, the number of stages of learning covered, the number of children who can use them at any time, the length of time which a child will require to work his way through the series and the durability of the materials, it is impossible to relate cost to use and so decide whether the books or equipment represent value for money. For example, a reading scheme of which the price may initially appear exorbitant, might include so much supporting material in the form of small story books, dictionaries, workcards, games and activities, that the need for additional extraneous materials would be greatly reduced. An alternative scheme or series of half-a-dozen books which may seem much cheaper could eventually prove more expensive, if it covered so little ground that its potentialities would be exhausted in a short space of time, and if large quantities of other materials would be required to make up for its deficiencies.

Certain sets of apparatus and equipment, particularly those which have been planned to cover a wide field in detailed developmental stages, and which are also well produced in a sturdy and attractive form, usually involve large initial outlays. The *S.R.A. Reading Laboratories* (Parker 1958) illustrate this point. Many head teachers may, quite understandably, hesitate about committing themselves to such a heavy outlay. A purchase of this nature, however, needs to be viewed against the wide amount of tuition it will provide for a great number of children over many years. Even then, the cost of a large expensive set of apparatus or cards can be virtually wasted if the various games and components are spread throughout so many classes that a particular piece of equipment in the series is not available for the child who has completed the preceding stage.

In general, the most expensive books and other reading equipment are those which will do little to further the child's reading progress and which he will have used and discarded in a very short time. Although there can be little to commend the purchase of most reading equipment which fulfils these criteria, an exception might be made in the case of certain books. Some of the earliest picture books which children use are quite expensive and may only be used for a short space of time. Yet if they serve to inculcate in children a love of books, their cost may well be justified.

3. The Use of Reading Materials

It is no part of the aim of this book to consider how all the different reading materials mentioned should be used. On the other hand, it is worth noting that much of the time and thought which goes into the teacher's assessment and selection of them can be wasted if the materials are not used to the best advantage once they have been purchased. To obtain the best use of any reading materials necessitates utilizing the entire scheme or set and using it, in the first instance, as the author intended.

Most, although not all, authors and inventors of reading books and other equipment have spent long months or years in perfecting their products. Often they have tried out, revised and discarded many ideas or items before the final product was accepted for publication. Many know, from their original experiments of using the earliest versions of the materials with children, how the best results can be obtained with their materials, and they state this either in the form of instructions or suggestions in their teacher's manual.

Teachers are sometimes reluctant to read the teachers' manuals of materials which they are purchasing. It is hoped that this book may encourage them to read these manuals at least twice: first before deciding to order the materials and, secondly, when the materials have arrived in the school and they are about to use them for the first time. It is strongly to be recommended that when a teacher tries out a new set of reading materials she should closely follow the author's suggestions. Only by doing so can she give the materials a fair trial and expect to get the best out of them. It is extremely unlikely that, *in the first instance*, a teacher inexperienced in the use of these particular materials can do better with them than the author who has thought about them, worked with them and tried them out over a long period of time. This is not to say that an experienced teacher who has used new reading materials for some time according to the author's plan may not be able to adapt or even improve the procedures for the children in her own class. Nevertheless, the general rule of using reading materials initially as the author intended them to be used is the one most likely to produce optimum results.

SUGGESTIONS FOR FURTHER READING

An interesting chapter on the 'climate' of a school or class can be found in:

OBRIST, C. and PICKARD, P. M. (1967) *Time for Reading*, Teacher's Manual. London: Ginn.

The reader who would like information on developments in reading materials in the U.S.A. should refer to the following two publications:

WITTICK, M. L. (1968) 'Innovations in reading instruction for beginners.' In ROBINSON, H. M. (ed.) *Innovation and Change in Reading Instruction*. The Sixty-seventh Yearbook of the National Society for the Study of Education, Part 2. Chicago: Chicago University Press.

KERFOOT, J. F. (1965) *First Grade Reading Programmes*. Newark, Delaware: International Reading Association.

Reading schemes, their vocabularies and their usage, are discussed in general terms in:

DIACK, H. (1960) *Reading and the Psychology of Perception*, chapter 12 and Appendix 1. Nottingham: Skinner.

MOYLE, D. (1968) *The Teaching of Reading*, chapter 10 and Appendix 2. London: Ward Lock.

Reference lists of children's reading books with suggested interest levels and reading ages are produced at intervals by The National Book League, 7 Albemarle Street, London W.1. For example:

DANIELS, J. C. and SEGAL, S. S. (1966) *Help in Reading: Books for the Teacher of Backward Children and for Pupils Backward in Reading.* London: The National Book League.

The following pamphlet also provides guidance for teachers 'on the selection of books for children which are appropriate to their individual interests and abilities', by suggesting reading age ranges and interest age ranges of reading books and reference books for both primary and secondary pupils:

LAWSON, K. S. (1968) *Children's Reading*, Paper No. 8. Leeds: The University of Leeds Institute of Education.

In the following publication, compiled by a committee of teachers of backward children, books for backward readers are appraised in more detail. As well as an assessment of reading ages and interest levels, comments are made about the covers, illustrations, type, vocabulary, style and contents of the books:

PASCOE, T. W. (ed.) (1962) *A Second Survey of Books for Backward Readers.* London: University of London Press.

Helpful information about the use of children's reading books and reference books can be found in the following two books, both of which contain particularly useful lists of sources from which information and help regarding choice of books can be obtained:

KAMM, A. and TAYLOR, B. (1966) *Books and the Teacher.* London: University of London Press.

CUTFORTH, J. A. and BATTERSBY, S. H. (1962) *Children and Books.* Oxford: Basil Blackwell.

7 Summary of criteria for assessing reading approaches

1. The Need for a Framework

In the preceding four chapters attention has been drawn to the many factors influencing reading progress, and it has been suggested that in selecting an approach to reading the teacher needs to make three main decisions. In the course of doing so she will have considered a large number of points, asked herself many questions and arrived at various answers.

In this chapter a list is provided of the main points put forward in chapters 3 to 6, as being important in the assessment of reading approaches. It is presented mainly in the form of questions which the teacher needs to ask. It is hoped that it will serve two useful functions: first, it will represent a summary of the criteria of assessment comprising Part 2 of this book; and, secondly, it will provide a framework for the examination of nine current reading approaches in Part 3, as well as for other approaches the teacher may wish to appraise.

2. Summary of Points Requiring Consideration

A. THE TEACHER

1. What are the teacher's basic beliefs about children's acquisition of reading skill? Do these beliefs lean towards systematic teaching or towards incidental learning?

2.   What is the teacher's preferred role? Does she see herself as a consultant and counsellor in the background or rather as a leader in the foreground, initiating instruction and learning?

3.   What are the classroom procedures in which the teacher believes and which she prefers to adopt, for example:

a.   a formal or informal régime;

b.   children working in large groups, small groups or individually;

c.   an early or delayed beginning to reading;

d.   dependence on one reading scheme, use of a number of reading schemes or no scheme at all;

e.   pre-choice and organization of reading materials by the teacher or freedom of selection by the children;

f.   reading closely integrated with spoken and written language or not;

g.   reading tuition confined to definite periods of the timetable or integrated informally and incidentally throughout most of the activities of the day?

4.   Which medium does the teacher support for beginning reading: t.o., a simplified spelling system such as i.t.a., or a coding system such as a colour code or system of diacritical marking?

5.   Which main method does the teacher prefer for beginning reading: a look-and-say approach or a phonic approach?

B.   THE SITUATION

1.   In what type of school or educational institution is the reading to take place: for example, an infant school, primary school, secondary school, special school, child guidance centre, remedial centre, evening institute or hospital?

2.   In what sort of area is the building situated? Is it in a deprived area or a high socio-economic area? Is it industrial or rural?

3.   What are the physical conditions in which the reading tuition is to be undertaken? Is the room small or large? Is it a confined space, is there opportunity to spread beyond one room or is it an open-plan school? Is there sufficient space to permit the adoption of the teacher's preferred procedures?

4. What sort of furniture and equipment are available?
5. How many children form the teaching unit?

C. THE CHILDREN

What are the characteristics and needs, both as a group and as individuals of the children with whom the approach will be used?

I. THE GROUP

a. What is the size of the group?
b. What is the composition of the group?
    i. Is the group heterogeneous or homogeneous in terms of chronological age, reading age and range of intelligence?
    ii. Does the group consist of both sexes?
    iii. What is the general socio-economic and educational background of the children in the group?

2. INDIVIDUAL CHILDREN

What are the individual needs of each child?
a. What is his age, intelligence, interests and abilities in reading?
b. Is his ability in oral language sufficiently developed to ensure the possibility of reading progress?
c. Does he have a preferred method of working, such as in short, sharp bursts or for long, concentrated periods?
d. Has he any physical or personality defects likely to handicap his progress in reading?

D. THE READING MATERIALS

I. THE AUTHOR

a. Has the author written a teacher's manual for the reading scheme or instructions for using the apparatus?

b. What are the basic beliefs of the author and are they in line with those of the teacher?

c. What is the role which the author assumes the teacher will adopt and what are the procedures he expects her to follow? Do these assumptions correspond with the teacher's preferences?

d. What is the author's background of experience?

e. What have other people to say concerning the author's ideas and how they work out in practice?

2.   THE MEDIUM AND METHOD EMPLOYED

Are the medium in which the reading materials are printed and the methods which underlie their construction those of which the teacher approves?

3.   CHILDREN FOR WHOM THE MATERIALS ARE APPROPRIATE

a. For exactly which children were the reading materials planned? The age, intelligence, linguistic competence, home background, interests and so on which the author had in mind are all important. Whether the materials were originally planned for retarded readers or for children making normal progress must also be considered.

b. Do the children with whom the teacher is thinking of using the materials resemble, in most of the preceding respects, the children for whom the materials were planned?

c. If the children in the proposed group differ greatly from those for whom the materials were designed, can the materials or ways of using them be satisfactorily adapted?

4.   OPTIMUM SITUATIONS

a. In which situations did the author contemplate the reading materials being used? The particular situation, the physical conditions and the educational 'climate' are relevant features of the situation.

b. Are these same conditions prevalent in the teacher's class or group?

c. If not, is it likely that the best use will be made of the reading materials in different situations?

5.   SCOPE OF THE MATERIALS

a.   Are the reading materials planned to form a complete reading scheme or intended as supplementary materials?
b.   If the materials are supplementary, what are they intended to supplement?
c.   If the materials are intended to represent a complete scheme, do they really achieve this?
d.   What is the scope of the materials in terms of initial and final levels of difficulty, and the gradient of progression within these two levels?

6.   STRUCTURAL AND FUNCTIONAL COMPETENCE

There are two related questions regarding competence.
a.   Does an examination of the structure of the materials show that the author has devised them in a technically competent manner? Examples of questions relating to structural competence are as follows:
>   *i.* What is the gradient of the introduction of new words or rules?
>   *ii.* Is there adequate repetition of new words and rules?
>   *iii.* Are there sufficient supplementary materials to encourage recognition of newly introduced words or to provide practice in the application of new rules?
>   *iv.* Is the sentence structure and flow of the prose designed to further understanding?

b.   Will the materials prove functionally effective; in other words, will they work? If they are used as suggested, with the appropriate children and in the expected situations, are the stated aims likely to be achieved?

7.   PRODUCTION OF THE MATERIALS

a.   Is the size and format of the books appropriate? Consider the appearance of the paper, print and covers. Are the books and apparatus durable, easy for the child to handle, easy to pack away and display?
b.   Are the illustrations attractive and appropriate? Do they fulfil a teaching function in relation to the text or are they solely decorative additions to the books?

8. EXCELLENCE

a. Has the author displayed more than just competence, by devising something which is original, imaginative, absolutely appropriate, inspirational or of high literary merit?
b. Has the author's special flair been supported by sensitive or exciting illustrations and high publishing standards, to produce reading materials of real merit or excellence?

9. COST

a. What is the actual cost of purchasing the complete scheme or set of materials?
b. What will be the relative cost? This is a more important question than the actual cost and not easy to determine. Questions such as the following need to be considered:
   i. What is the scope of the scheme?
   ii. What quantity of materials does it comprise?
   iii. For how many children will it cater and for what length of time?

E. APPARATUS

The selection of reading apparatus poses special problems for the teacher. Many of the preceding points relating to reading materials apply equally well to the selection of apparatus as to books, but the following additional points merit consideration in respect of reading apparatus.

1. What is the precise purpose, in terms of learning to read, of the particular game or piece of apparatus? Is it intended as a tool for teaching, for reinforcing learning or for practising a newly acquired skill?

2. Will the reading progress of the child who is to use the apparatus or play the game actually be helped or will he merely be kept occupied?

3. Is the apparatus part of a complete scheme, a supplement to some other scheme or a discrete piece of apparatus? If it is not part of a complete scheme, will it prove a useful supplement to the teacher's reading programme?

4. Will it take the teacher a long time both to prepare the apparatus before it can be used and to store it away after use? Alternatively, are pieces clearly marked and containers provided so that children can be responsible for the distribution, collection and storage of the apparatus?

5. Are the pieces which make up the whole, attractive, appropriate in size and durable?

6. Are there clear instructions for the teacher's benefit, regarding how the apparatus should be used or the game played?

7. Are the rules which the children have to follow sufficiently simple and clear?

8. Is the apparatus self-checking?

F. FOOTNOTE

In order to make the best use of reading materials of every kind, it is wise to purchase the entire reading scheme or set of apparatus and, in the first instance, to use it as the author intended it to be used.

PART THREE
An Examination of Nine Current
Approaches to Reading

8 Look-and-say approaches

The majority of basic reading schemes published in Great Britain during the 1950's and 1960's employed a look-and-say method. The following are examples of such schemes: *The Pilot Reading Scheme* (Davenport 1953), *The Happy Trio* (Gray 1956), *The McKee Readers* (McKee 1956), *Let's Learn To Read* (Taylor and Ingleby 1960), *Key Words Reading Scheme* (Murray 1964), *Queensway Reading* (Brearley and Neilson 1964), *Ready to Read* (Simpson 1966) and *Time for Reading* (Obrist and Pickard 1967).

Two of these schemes, *Queensway Reading* and *Key Words Reading Scheme*, both published in 1964, form a contrast to each other. In *Queensway Reading* a look-and-say sentence method is used with a strong emphasis on a story approach. *Key Words Reading Scheme*, which begins with a look-and-say word method and includes both written work and phonic work, is more eclectic in its approach. In the former scheme, the emphasis is on learning while the latter leans more towards teaching. A third scheme, *Time for Reading*, published in 1967, is one which can easily be adapted by the teacher who wishes to place the emphasis on either learning or teaching. In fact, this scheme is divided into sections, each of which can be used effectively in a variety of ways. An examination of these three contrasting schemes, in the ways suggested in Part 2 of this book, will illustrate how other look-and-say reading schemes might be appraised.

1. Queensway Reading
(Brearley, M. and Neilson, L., 1964)

A. THE AUTHORS

I.   BACKGROUND

The two authors of *Queensway Reading*, Molly Brearley and Lois Neilson, are both experienced and knowledgeable in the field of infant education. Molly Brearley is Principal of the Froebel Educational Institute and Lois Neilson is headmistress of a primary school.

2.   BASIC BELIEFS

According to the terms used in this book, the author's beliefs are centred on incidental learning. These beliefs can be said to represent 'the Froebel approach to learning', with its emphasis on the child's learning, his needs and all-round development, rather than on the isolation and specific teaching of the skill of reading. The teacher is regarded as a consultant rather than as an instructor or leader.

Two particular aspects of the authors' beliefs about learning to read are emphasized in the manual. They regard reading as part of communication and language development and state: 'A child learns to speak by being with people who are speaking and who include him in their communications; a child's reading can come in the same way.' The authors also stress that they wish the books to be 'instruments of thinking and feeling'. They believe that 'Too often children's early reading material is devoid of feeling.' They go on to suggest that '. . . all children experience loneliness, fun, excitement, compassion, fear, creative satisfaction, the wish to grow up, the temptation to do forbidden things, the need for family solidarity, losing and forgetting things, little triumphs and disasters – and so do the children in these stories.' The authors assert that even in Book One of *Queensway Reading* they ask more of the children than merely 'reading the words'; they want reactions in terms of thought and association.

3. TEACHER'S MANUAL

The teacher's manual contains a short general chapter on the teaching of reading, a bibliography for teachers who wish to pursue their own further study on this subject, descriptions of the items which comprise *Queensway Reading* and suggestions on how they might be used. In addition, there are vocabulary lists showing exactly which new words are introduced in each book and a complete word analysis giving the number of occurrences of every word in all the books in which it appears. In short, in the teacher's manual the authors have avoided the temptation to be verbose on the subject of reading in general and have given, very concisely, their main beliefs about reading, together with clear details of how the scheme has been built up and how it might be used. Consequently, any teacher who is prepared to spend an hour or two in studying this manual should experience no difficulty whatsoever in deciding whether or not *Queensway Reading* is an approach which she wishes to use with her group of children.

B. MEDIUM AND METHOD

The medium employed in *Queensway Reading* is t.o., and the method a global one, namely look-and-say sentence method.

C. THE SCOPE OF THE SCHEME

I. A COMPLETE READING SCHEME

Queensway Reading is planned as a complete reading scheme comprising a teacher's manual, a book of stories for the teacher to read to the children, a children's picture dictionary, nine main reading books, twenty supplementary story books, wall pictures, picture cards, word cards and sentence cards.

2. RANGE OF READING ATTAINMENTS

The scheme begins with the earliest stage of beginning to read and extends to a level of attainment at which the child can read a continuous story of thirty-two pages, with a difficulty level equivalent to a reading age of approximately seven and a half to eight.

3. INTENDED PUPILS

A study of the teacher's manual and the pupils' materials suggests that the scheme is intended for infants, especially for groups of children within a 'progressive' infant school in which informal procedures are in force.

D. SPECIAL FEATURES OF THE SCHEME

1. CHILDREN'S SPOKEN VOCABULARY

The vocabulary of the reading books is based on the words from Burrough's (1957) lists of the spoken vocabulary of five- and six-year-olds.

2. A TEACHER'S BOOK OF STORIES

A special feature of the scheme is a book of stories for the teacher to read to the children before and during work with the children's reading books. These stories concern the chief characters to be found in the children's books, in particular Judy and her adopted brother, Robert, both aged five. Most of the stories relate to events before Judy and Robert begin school. The first story in the children's books provides continuity with the stories read by the teacher, as it relates to Judy and Robert's first day at school. The *Book of Stories* ensures that, before handling the reading books, the children in a group will gain a common background of interest and experience in the spoken vocabulary which will form the printed vocabulary of their first reading books. In addition, as the children will have discussed the stories and their related pictures with their teacher and with each other, common bonds of communication will have been established.

3. THE SCHEME CONSISTS ENTIRELY OF STORIES

The twenty-nine children's books all consist entirely of stories. In this context it should be noted that in the early stages of any look-and-say reading scheme, when repetition of a comparatively small number of words is essential, it is extremely difficult for authors to produce real stories instead of merely stilted sentences strung together round a topic. The authors of *Queensway Reading* state that 'Within the necessary limitations of vocabulary, especially in the earlier stages, the highest degree of spontaneity and appeal has been aimed at in the reading material. Necessary repetition has been carefully controlled so that it does not become obtrusive and "kill" the story.' These claims are substantiated when one reads the stories in the children's books. Even in Book One there is a story which moves forward naturally from the initial introduction of the characters towards a satisfactory conclusion. It is not simply a collection of sentences achieved by juggling a limited number of words in varying combinations. On the other hand, in this first book, the teacher may well have to help young children to make the necessary transition from one situation to another, for example from outside the school on page 16 to inside the classroom on page 17, by discussing the sequence of events with them.

E. ADDITIONAL DETAILS

1. VOCABULARY

The vocabulary content of the scheme comprises about 1,155 different basic words, excluding variants. If the variants employed are also included, for example the words 'goes', 'going' and 'gone', as well as the word 'go', the effective total of words is nearer 1,500. The Vocabulary List for Book One, the first children's book* published in 1964, lists seventy-nine words, but if plurals and apostrophe 's' are not counted as separate words, the total would be sixty-one. A teacher who might wonder if sixty-one words is too many for a first reading book needs to bear in mind that the children will be familiar with the spoken form of many of the words, phrases and sentences through the stories read to them by the

---

* Three additional children's books were published in 1966 and 1967, as follows:
'Robert and Judy' – *Queensway Reading Introductory Book* (1966)
'Poppett and Squeakie' – *Queensway Reading Inter 1:2* (1967)
'Where Are They? – *Queensway Reading Inter 2:3* (1967)

teacher and through other pre-reading activities. The total of new words should also be related to the frequency of repetition of words: the Word Analysis in the teacher's manual shows an extensive repetition of words spread over many books. It should also be remembered that, if interesting stories are aimed at in the initial stages of learning to read, they cannot be achieved within the framework of tiny vocabularies. On the other hand, the publication of three additional children's books in this scheme, to precede Book One and fit in between Stages 1 and 2, and Stages 2 and 3, suggests that some children may have found the vocabulary content of the first three basic books to represent too steep a gradient of difficulty. The introduction of these three new books should help to relieve any anxieties teachers may have felt regarding the previous vocabulary loading. (The vocabulary of *Queensway Reading* is compared with the vocabulary of other look-and-say schemes in the Appendix.)

2. SUPPORTIVE MATERIALS

Queensway Reading is well provided with a variety of equipment for use by both the teacher and the children, in different pre-reading activities. The equipment lends itself to being utilized by the teacher according to her own ideas or, if she prefers, she can follow the helpful suggestions for its use given in the teacher's manual.

3. CONTENT OF STORIES

The stories in the nine basic books are concerned with Robert and Judy aged five; their everyday activities such as going to school, shopping, visiting the station or the seaside, as well as more exciting episodes involving other people. The home-background of the two children is middle class. The complementary books for the first two stages also consist of stories about the same two children. However, by Stage 3, although Robert and Judy still feature in certain stories, in other books they are not mentioned. For example, nine of the complementary books for Stages 3 to 6 are about a robin, a bus, a donkey, two Koala bears, a flying horse and various other children. This introduction of stories centred on entirely different characters is likely to provide increased enjoyment and stimulation for the child who has mastered the initial stages of reading and who can sometimes become weary of reading about the same characters in an endless succession of books.

4. FORMAT

The covers of each basic book are a different colour, and the covers of the complementary books at each stage match the basic books, thus simplifying identification. Linson cloth is used for the covers of the basic books and card for the complementary books. The pages of all the books are stapled together instead of being stitched.

5. THE PRINT

The type used in the books is clear and pleasing, and the script 'a' and 'g' is used throughout.

6. EARLY PHRASING

Right from the first page the text consists of complete sentences which have about them the ring of children's authentic speech. Although the text is printed as prose, in the early books the phrasing of each line of print has been carefully devised to present a visually meaningful linguistic pattern. The needs of the children and the requirements of the language, as envisaged by the authors, have clearly not been sacrificed to the typesetter's urge to fill up each line of print. The following example from Book One will suffice as an illustration:

This is the way
we go to school.

In the above sentence there was sufficient space at the end of the first line for the word 'we' to have been included. However, a space at the end of the line was obviously preferred in order to present the child with a meaningful phrase on each line of print.

7. ILLUSTRATIONS

The basic books are attractively illustrated in full colour, while the complementary books have two-colour illustrations. The illustrations also serve a teaching function. The authors say, 'The large variety of colourful pictures have been included not only to attract the child to the books but also to help him in his recognition of the words.' The introduction of the word 'sand' in Book One will serve as an example to support their statement. An illustration shows a teacher, with two children beside her, leaning over a sand tray. The text below this picture reads as follows:

> Would you like to play
> in the sand?
> What would you like
> to make with the sand?

In similar manner, throughout the early books, the pictures help to tell the story while serving to suggest, or remind, the child of the relevant words.

8. RELATIONSHIP WITH CHILDREN'S WRITING

The selection of a reading scheme may, to some extent, be related to the teacher's beliefs about children's writing. The teacher who is convinced that children's free writing plays an important part in the development of the language arts may be looking for a reading scheme likely to encourage children's spontaneous writing. Such a teacher may consider that the imaginative stories in *Queensway Reading*, with their emphasis on thinking and feeling, could be instrumental in fostering creative writing.

F. OPTIMUM SITUATIONS

Situations in which *Queensway Reading* would be likely to be used to the best advantage would incorporate many of the following features:

1. children aged five to seven years;
2. children who are of average or above average intelligence rather

than of low intelligence, and who come from homes of average or above average socio-economic level;

3. a teacher whose basic beliefs about reading are centred on learning rather than teaching and who considers the child's all-round development to be more important than the acquisition of reading skill;

4. a teacher who prefers the role of a consultant to that of a leader;

5. a teacher who prefers to delay rather than hasten the beginning of reading tuition but who is prepared actively to encourage reading readiness by reading stories to children and by emphasizing speaking and listening in other ways, and at a later stage, by associating the spoken language with the printed or hand-written words;

6. a modern classroom in which children have opportunities and encouragement to move about, engage in various activities and talk to each other and to the teacher – that is, informal rather than formal procedures in a flexible and well-equipped environment.

2. Key Words Reading Scheme
(Murray, W., 1964)

A. THE AUTHOR

I. BACKGROUND

W. Murray, the author of *Key Words Reading Scheme*, was headmaster of a special school for educationally sub-normal children at the time when the scheme was written, but the majority of his many years of teaching experience have been with normal children. He is also co-author with McNally of *Key Words to Literacy* (1962).

2. BASIC BELIEFS

Although this is a look-and-say scheme, the author's emphasis on the importance of mastering the most frequently used words of our language

during the early stages of reading suggests that his beliefs should be classified as supporting the basic philosophy of systematic tuition rather than
that of incidental learning.

3. TEACHER'S MANUAL

There is no teacher's manual to the scheme but a brief pamphlet entitled
Notes for Teachers can be obtained from the publishers, free of cost. It
describes all the reading materials which form part of the scheme, gives a
list of the number of new words introduced in each book and suggests
levels of reading ages.

B. MEDIUM AND METHOD

The medium employed in *Key Words Reading Scheme* is t.o. The scheme is
based primarily on a global method, making use of both words and
sentences in the early stages. However, as the scheme commences with
discrete words, and as new words are isolated at the bottom of each page
on which they are introduced, it should be classified as beginning with a
look-and-say word method. As the scheme also introduces phonic work
and written exercises it represents an eclectic approach to reading.

C. THE SCOPE OF THE SCHEME

I. A COMPLETE READING SCHEME

Key Words Reading Scheme is planned as a complete reading scheme
consisting of a set of notes for the teacher, thirty-six children's reading
books, children's workbooks, large and small flash cards, outline picture
pads, picture-word matching cards, picture sentence cards, large wall
pictures with sentence strips and two picture dictionaries. The children's
books comprise three parallel sets of twelve books each. The 'a' book at
each level is the basic reading book, 'b' is a supplementary reading book,
while 'c' introduces written exercises and, from Book 4c onwards, phonic
work.

2. RANGE OF READING ATTAINMENTS

The scheme is intended for the beginning reader and it is suggested in the teacher's pamphlet that it extends from a reading age of four to a reading age of ten. This suggested range of reading ages may be rather wide. Probably a more realistic estimate would be an average reading age of about seven at the level of Book 9 and a reading age of eight to eight and a half on completion of the scheme.

3. INTENDED PUPILS

In contrast to *Queensway Reading*, this scheme is not intended primarily for infants. The ages of the two children round whom the incidents centre are not specified but one might guess them to be about nine and seven years old. Illustrations of these two children show them as neither too old for infants to be able to identify themselves with them nor yet so young that older pupils would regard them as too babyish to merit interest. Consequently this reading scheme is likely to be found acceptable for use with a wide age range including infants, children of junior-school age and even possibly children in the lower forms of secondary schools.

D. SPECIAL FEATURES OF THE SCHEME

I. KEY WORDS

McNally and Murray (1962) carried out a piece of research which resulted in the selection of 200 key words which 'account for half to three-quarters of the running words occurring in everyday reading matter'. The first twelve key words make up a quarter of the words we read and write; the first thirty basic words account for one-third of the words we normally read; one hundred words make up half of those in common use. Such a finding is obviously of great importance in the initial stages of learning to read and write. The *Key Words Reading Scheme* utilizes the findings of this research and emphasizes 300 'key words'. Accordingly it is likely to ease children's difficulties in beginning reading and bring them more rapidly to the point at which they can attempt to read for themselves books they have chosen from the book corner.

E. ADDITIONAL DETAILS

1. VOCABULARY

The information which is provided for the teacher inside the covers of each book includes lists of the new words introduced in the book, as well as details of the average repetition of words and total vocabulary load in the text. The publisher's pamphlet relating to *Key Words Reading Scheme* states that: 'The scheme starts with fewer words than any other reading scheme, so that the learner can make a rapid, confident and often earlier start.' Book 1a utilizes only sixteen different words with an average of ten repetitions per word. Books 1b and 1c use exactly the same sixteen words. The second book introduces twenty-seven new words, the third thirty-six new words and so on at this very gradual gradient, combined with an extremely high rate of repetition of words and, in the first six books, a total carry-over of words from one book to the next. By Book 8a, ninety-two new words are introduced and, at this stage, all 300 key words have been used within a total of 377 words. As the children who have progressed this far in the scheme will have read twenty-four books, it undoubtedly offers an exceptionally gentle gradient of difficulty in the initial stages of learning to read. The remaining books add 503 new words to make up a total vocabulary load of 880 words (with certain additional phonic words), for the entire reding scheme.

(The vocabulary of *Key Words Reading Scheme* is compared with the vocabulary of other look-and-say schemes in the Appendix.)

2. SUPPORTIVE MATERIALS

The variety of attractive apparatus which is provided permits the teacher to arrange for different pre-reading activities in accordance with her own ideas. Much of the apparatus will also be found valuable for reinforcement of learning as the child progresses through the reading scheme.

The Key Words Cards, which are suggested for use with Books 3 to 8, form a simple and particularly useful piece of apparatus which will help children to write and spell the key words which they are learning to read. One of these cards, when laid flat, shows all 200 key words set out alphabetically for easy reference. Coloured illustrations of some of the key words are presented on the back cover. The modest price of these cards should make it a practical proposition for every child to keep one permanently by him for easy reference.

The 'c' book at each level utilizes exactly the same words as the 'a' and 'b' book. It is intended to provide the link between reading and writing and, from Book 4c onwards, to introduce phonics. Yet it seems doubtful whether the 'c' series of books can actually be considered as parallel to the 'a' and 'b' series at each level. The written exercises in the early 'c' books appear rather difficult and the phonic work in the later books too simple for children who will have read the appropriate 'a' and 'b' books.

For example, Books 1c, 2c and 3c include three types of written exercises; completing a word within a sentence when the initial letter of the word is given, reading questions and answering them with 'Yes' or 'No' and sorting out jumbled sentences. The third exercise of jumbled sentences is one which children even of seven and eight years old quite often find particularly difficult. The experienced teacher of five-year-olds will no doubt ask herself if these children, even when they can read Books 1a and 1b and recognize the sixteen words by sight, will be able to undertake the three different types of exercises found in Book 1c.

The phonic training, commencing in Book 4c, is by contrast quite simple. It begins by emphasizing the sound 'c' which comes at the beginning of the known words 'car' 'cow', 'cat' and 'cake'; it then continues in a similar manner with other initial letters of known words. By Book 9c such simple beginning of words as 'sp' and 'tr' and endings like '...y' and '...le' are being introduced. Yet, at the identical level of 9a in the basic reading books the author suggests that children's reading ages will be eight to eight and a half years. Children who have progressed through the reading scheme will have a sight vocabulary of 487 words and their next reading book in the scheme will be an adventure tale of twenty-four pages of fairly close print, introducing 115 new words. Teachers may doubt whether a child who is reading fluently at this level requires his attention to be drawn to the sound of '...ed' in the words 'picked', 'cooked' and 'stopped', and other similar, simple phonic rules.

The problem of 'pacing' the 'c' series of books, comprising written work and phonic training, was evidently difficult and it seems doubtful if it was satisfactorily solved. Nevertheless, teachers who do not consider the 'c' series of books to be appropriate at the levels indicated may consider them of value for certain children in selected situations. Moreover, some teachers who like to establish a fairly solid basis of phonic rules may prefer to plan their own phonic training alongside the 'a' and 'b' reading books. In neither case need reservations concerning the usefulness of the 'c' books detract from the value and appeal of the parallel sets of 'a' and 'b' reading books.

3. CONTENT OF STORIES

The subject matter of both the 'a' and 'b' books relates to the activities of Peter and Jane, their family, relatives and friends. The family owns a car and their status is clearly of average or above average socio-economic level. Each of the first nine books, in both the 'a' and 'b' series, is made up of a series of episodes in the children's daily life rather than of complete stories, each with a beginning and a sequence of developmental actions which lead to an ultimate conclusion. In other words the books relate to various incidents in children's lives, in contrast to the sequential stories which constitute *Queensway Reading*. The titles of Book 3a – *Things We Like* – and Book 9a – *Games We Like* – give some idea of this system of the grouping together of incidents to make a book. Book 7a, entitled *Happy Holiday*, is concerned entirely with the children's stay with an aunt and uncle at the seaside and so more nearly approaches a complete story. Yet here again, most of the reading matter consists of a compilation of daily events described in the present tense. The material in the first nine books is descriptive rather than imaginative and is, therefore, perhaps unlikely to induce reflective reading.

An adult reading straight through the first nine books at one sitting might be struck by a sameness about the events, various combinations of the following episodes appearing in most of the books: playing with toys, playing in water and with boats, having tea, shopping, visiting relatives and so on. Yet the child who is reading these books over a period of time may regard them differently. The teacher assessing the content of the reading books needs to remind herself that a look-and-say word method usually results in material which is more stilted in the early stages than a look-and-say sentence method. It should further be borne in mind that, if books are to use only a very small vocabulary and if each word has to be repeated literally dozens of times, it is impossible to devise continuous stories with a wide variety of subject matter played out against different backgrounds. A very limited vocabulary, accompanied by frequent repetition of words planned to help the child to acquire a basic sight vocabulary easily and surely, must inevitably result in the subject matter being merely variations on similar themes. Working within the limits of this strictly controlled vocabulary, the author has shown great ingenuity and clearly demonstrated his intimate knowledge of children by devising episodes likely to interest them.

Books 10a, 11a and 12a, with the titles *Adventure on the Island*, *Mystery of the Island* and *The Holiday Camp Mystery* move into the realm of real story books. Two cousins who are 'a lot older than Peter and Jane' are introduced. The illustrations show the two cousins to be boys of about sixteen and eighteen. Each of these three books comprises a complete story likely to be of interest to junior and secondary-modern school children. Certain infant teachers may consider that their pupils, after reaching Book 9, would benefit from reading other stories, such as simple folk tales which would offer them a variety of different characters, in preference to proceeding to the final three stages of the scheme with their older interest level.

4. FORMAT

The thirty-six children's books in *Key Words Reading Scheme* are all exactly the same size and have the usual 'Ladybird' format with which many children are familiar even before they start school, through buying 'Ladybird' books of different kinds in bookshops. The books are sturdy, having stitched bindings set in hard backs with a full-colour, full-size illustration on the front cover of each. To aid identification, the spines and backs of the books in the three series are in three distinctive colours and there are clear numbers and titles on the spines and fronts of the books. All the books contain full-colour illustrations, so that each page of print is opposite a full-page picture.

5. THE PRINT

The first book is printed in very large script letters, the capital letters being about half an inch (13 mm) high. In the following five books the print decreases in size with every book, while the number of words per page increases. Books 7 to 12 employ a uniform size of print and discontinue the use of the script 'a' and 'g'.

6. EARLY PHRASING

Book 1a commences with single words and phrases, which are soon replaced by sentences. Owing to the large size of print, not more than three words can be printed on one line, so that it has not always been possible to present one line of print as a linguistically meaningful phrase. In Book 2a, with its somewhat smaller print, the author has managed to space meaningful phrases on separate lines. Yet, rather strangely, in Book 3a, in which the size of print is further reduced and thus more space is available, this policy has not been continued. One finds sentences breaking at the end of a line with a preposition or conjunction, for example:

> Peter and Jane are at
> the station.

This sentence could have presented the child with two much more **mean-ingful** phrases if it had been spaced as follows:

> Peter and Jane
> are at the station.

One also wonders why, in this book, when a sentence is split between two lines, the last two words are placed at the very end of a line of print rather than near the beginning of the line. The young child in an early stage of learning to read sometimes fails to notice words so situated.

7. ILLUSTRATIONS

To both children and their teachers, the large colourful illustrations found throughout the books and supportive materials of the *Key Words Reading Scheme* represent one of its most appealing features. The pictures certainly attract children to the books, give pleasure when they are more closely examined, and contribute to the child's motivation regarding learning to read. Thus one of the important functions of illustrations, namely to attract children to the books, is undoubtedly achieved. The other purpose of illustrations – to serve a teaching function – has not been served. The reason is to be found mainly in the basic structure of the scheme itself.

The employment of a very small vocabulary which is increased only gradually, although it eases the learning burden for children also carries with it certain handicaps. One, already mentioned, is that incidents and stories in the text are bound to be somewhat stilted. The same handicap would apply to the illustrations if they referred literally to the text, particularly in the early stages. The author and the illustrators obviously found themselves in a quandary here. Had the pictures been designed to serve a teaching function and merely illustrated the text, they would have been unavoidably dull and repetitive and consequently unlikely to stimulate children. In order to avoid this situation, attractive illustrations likely to capture children's interest have been provided, with the inevitable result that these illustrations can rarely be used as teaching tools. In other words, the pictures are extrinsic rather than intrinsic to the process of learning to read.

While illustrations extrinsic to a reading scheme can provide greater initial attraction for children than many intrinsic illustrations, they do have two drawbacks. In the first instance, attractive illustrations can mislead the child about the content of the story, for, with a small controlled vocabulary, children may find that the actual reading material comes as an anticlimax after the pictures. Secondly, and this is probably more important, the illustrations can suggest to the child words he expects to find on the printed page but which are not there. For example, the illustration opposite page 12 in Book 1a shows Peter and Jane, dressed as Red Indians, peeping out of a wigwam. A child seeing this picture might expect to read the words, 'Peter and Jane are Red Indians', or 'Peter and Jane are in a wigwam'. Instead, the text opposite reads, 'Here is Peter and here is Jane'. Similarly, opposite page 26 we see Jane skipping. A child might suppose the relevant sentence to be 'Jane is skipping'; in fact it is 'I like Jane'.

It all depends on the teacher's priorities in criteria of assessment. If she wants a scheme to be based on a small vocabulary load, she can either have with it rather dull and somewhat repetitive pictures which guide the child to make correct responses to the printed words or she can have varied and lively pictures which do not fulfil a teaching function. The teacher who chooses *Key Words Reading Scheme* because of its easy gradient of difficulty and its lavish illustrations, and is aware of the problem posed by the relationship of text and illustration, can take necessary precautions. She can, for instance, exercise direct control over the child's earliest reading by ensuring that she herself always pronounces the actual printed words before the child speaks words which are not in the text.

8.   RELATIONSHIP WITH CHILDREN'S FREE WRITING

The 'c' series of books introduces children to written exercises, using the words they have been reading in the 'a' and 'b' books at the same stage. Many teachers, however, may be equally or more interested in the question of how a reading scheme is likely to encourage children's free writing. They will find that the relationship between *Key Words Reading Scheme* and children's free writing differs somewhat from that noted with *Queensway Reading*. The stories in *Key Words Reading Scheme*, being more factual and descriptive, are less likely to trigger off imaginative free writing than the stories in *Queensway Reading*. On the other hand, many of the colourful illustrations in *Key Words Reading Scheme* (for example the first three pictures in Book 1b, showing children examining a rock pool and butterflies) could quite easily inspire some children to make up stories about the pictures and then want to write them. Furthermore, if the illustrations in the books or the activities of home or school are such as to encourage children's free writing, children who have learnt to read and write 'key words' would find themselves at a great advantage from the viewpoint of mastery of the most commonly used words in our language.

F.   OPTIMUM SITUATIONS

Certain features of *Key Words Reading Scheme* render it appropriate in a greater variety of situations than many schemes for beginning reading.

For example, whilst *Queensway Reading* is more suitable for infants, *Key Words Reading Scheme* with its low vocabulary load, gentle gradient of introduction of new words, frequent repetition of words and also its illustrations of children older than infants can easily be adapted for use with older pupils as well as infants. Optimum situations for using this scheme will, accordingly, combine many of the following factors:

1. children who have not yet started school or who are in nursery schools and classes, and any other age of children from five to eleven or twelve years of age;

2. children of low intelligence, for example those in E.S.N. schools, as well as children of average and above-average intelligence;

3. probably children who come from homes of average or above-average socio-economic level;

4. a teacher who believes that reading is a skill which needs to be taught, who favours an early rather than a delayed beginning and who is prepared to instruct as well as guide;

5. either a formal or informal infant class, with groups of retarded readers in junior classes or secondary schools, in special schools, in remedial centres and with individual children at home, at child guidance clinics or in hospitals.

3. Time for Reading
(Obrist, C. and Pickard, P. M., 1967)

A. THE AUTHORS

I. BACKGROUND

Cecilia Obrist is the headmistress of an infant school and Phyllis Pickard was formerly Principal Lecturer in Education at Maria Grey College of Education. Both the authors have had long experience in the teaching of young children.

2. BASIC BELIEFS

The authors favour the basic belief of incidental learning. They believe that a child's interests are fundamentally important because they form the primary source of motivation for learning. Therefore they support the concepts of activity and informal teaching, whereby children are involved in a variety of activities, all of which impinge on learning to read. Throughout the scheme it is clear that the authors consider that an appropriate classroom climate and teacher-child participation form essential features of the early stages of learning to read.

3. TEACHER'S MANUAL

The teacher's manual falls into two parts. Part One gives some research findings and describes the development of pictorial and symbolic representation culminating in the creation of an alphabet. There is a stimulating chapter on the climate necessary for the unfettered development of reading ability. Part Two contains instructions for using the scheme. These instructions are given in unusual detail and they suggest ways in which a scheme of learning to read can be integrated with a full infant school programme of reading, writing, games, singing, art and craft. Incidentally, Part Two would form an excellent guide for a probationary teacher or for a teacher changing from a formal to an informal approach, particularly if she is not quite sure of how this can be done most effectively.

B. MEDIUM AND METHOD

The medium used in *Time for Reading* is t.o. 'A combination of methods' is suggested 'with the sentence method and look-and-say coming first, supported and extended by kinaesthesia'. This really means that the scheme relies heavily upon writing and drawing as aids to learning. There is also provision in both the reading books and apparatus for phonic work to be introduced incidentally. The result is that *Time for Reading* is even more of an eclectic approach to reading than *Key Words Reading Scheme*, and forms a marked contrast with *Queensway Reading*.

C. THE SCOPE OF THE SCHEME

I. A COMPLETE READING SCHEME

Time for Reading is planned as a complete reading scheme. It consists of a teacher's manual, a book of stories for the teacher to read to the children, and a sequence of apparatus, books and games. However, it is typical of the authors' broad concept of infant education that they suggest ways in which the scheme can be supplemented by books and materials from other schemes, if the progress of the child requires it.

2. RANGE OF READING ATTAINMENTS

The scheme begins with the earliest stage of beginning to read and extends to a level of attainment at which the child can read fluently with a reading age of approximately eight years.

3. INTENDED PUPILS

The suggestions in the teacher's manual and the contents of the scheme strongly indicate that the scheme is intended for infants, especially for children in an informal 'progressive' school.

D. SPECIAL FEATURES

I. A TEACHER'S BOOK OF STORIES

A teacher's story book, placed at the beginning of the scheme, is intended as an introduction to the basic elements in the stories which the children will read later. While in this respect it resembles *Queensway Reading*, *Time for Reading* goes further, as the teacher's story book is accompanied by a children's picture book. When the two are used together, the one by the teacher and the other by the child, they form an introduction to the use of books.

Some of the stories and poems are traditional. Others are based on the child's own problems and background interests, and their purpose is to introduce the Cherry family, with whom the stories in the reading books are concerned. All the stories read by the teacher are designed to involve the children, either in the repetitive parts of the traditional folk stories or in discussion about the family and their problems and interests.

The teacher's manual contains useful comments on ways in which these stories can be used. Suggestions for 'expanding' the stories to include other aspects of work in the 'progressive' infant classroom will appeal to many teachers.

2. THE WORKBOOKS

The authors of this scheme think that in learning to read the young child should learn through his kinaesthetic sense as well as through his visual and auditory senses. Accordingly, they have provided workbooks to accompany the first four stages of the scheme. These workbooks contain a wide range of activities: they begin with drawing, colouring and pattern making in the first book and progress through a series of writing, selecting, categorizing and reading exercises in the following books. In all these exercises the child has to think about what he is doing, rather than merely copy what he sees before him.

A further objective of these workbooks is to train the children to refer to the reading books in this scheme. Many of the exercises require the child to seek information from the appropriate story book and then to use that information. Teachers will find these workbooks an exciting extension of the reading scheme; although the work is pitched at a level within the capability of the normal child, the exercises make rigorous and exacting demands upon the child.

E. ADDITIONAL DETAILS

I. THE STRUCTURE OF THE SCHEME

The scheme is divided into seven stages. The first stage is a pre-reading stage in which the children listen to stories, follow the stories in their picture book and draw in the workbook. Thereafter, for the purposes of vocabulary control, the scheme is divided into thirty items, which include reading books, apparatus, games and workbooks.

2.   VOCABULARY

The vocabulary content of the scheme consists of 1,715 different words, and with the repetitions there are 17,300 words altogether. The gradient in the early stages of the scheme is gradual, but the most important feature concerning the introduction of new words is that the scheme is designed in such a way that all the twenty-seven items which comprise Stages 2 to 4 contribute to the learning of new words. This means that the child does not have to meet all the new words in the reading books. Some are learnt in the games and some through the apparatus. (The vocabulary of this scheme is compared with the vocabulary of other look-and-say schemes in the Appendix.)

Although *Time for Reading* employs a look-and-say method, the authors of the scheme accept the need for phonic instruction. They point out, however, that the teacher must decide when to introduce this type of instruction and they suggest that the *Six Phonic Workbooks* (Grassam 1965) could be used alongside work with *Time for Reading*.

3.   SUPPORTIVE MATERIALS

The apparatus consists of word and sentence cards, classroom labels, wall pictures, outline pictures for colouring, and several games of Lotto. There are many ways of using these pieces of apparatus, both as material supplementary to that which has been learnt and as devices for instigating new learning. The teacher's manual makes many interesting suggestions.

Unfortunately there is one note of reservation about the Lotto games. They are not progressive. The earlier and the later games follow the same pattern, in that the Lotto cards contain a picture and the corresponding word. It seems a pity that some of the later Lotto cards did not contain words only, so that the child would have to look for the word rather than the picture. It seems the height of optimism to expect the child to bother with words when a glance at a picture tells him all he needs to know. However, some teachers may think it worth while to write words on the reverse side of the cards and so make two games out of one piece of apparatus.

4.   CONTENT OF THE STORIES

There is an interesting and extremely well thought out progressive
pattern running through the eighteen story books. The first book, *The
Cherry Family*, introduces the family in the familiar setting of the home,
and it deals with various aspects of family life. Then comes a great occasion,
the child's birthday, and in particular the fifth birthday with all its implications of going to school and passing from babyhood to childhood.
Gradually, the stories begin to expand the child's reading environment.
He reads about cowboys, animals of other lands and a variety of interesting activities connected with his actual environment. In this way the
stories are intended to draw the child outwards from the family, which is
epitomized by the Cherry family, to a widening range of new ideas and
activities.

A noticeable feature in all these books is the skilful way in which
patterns of language, phrases and customary phraseology are repeated so
that the child becomes familiar with the visual representation of sentence
and phrase patterns. Similarly there is a regulated pattern in the introduction of words which conform to one another in their general structure.
For example in Book 3, which is really item number ten, the word 'gave'
is introduced on page 2, repeated on pages 3, 4, 5, and 6, so that it is well
implanted in the child's mind, and then the word 'came' is similarly dealt
with. Finally, on the last page another word of similar structure, 'home',
is introduced. All the books follow this practice of introducing words
which obey a rule and allowing the child to learn by comparing and
contrasting its elements. Ronald Morris has used the term 'learning by
contrastive discrimination' for this learning process. It is one of the ways
by which a child learns to talk.

5.   FORMAT

The covers of all the books differ, and they are decorated by the drawings
of children. Where possible these pictures convey the subject matter of the
contents. The thicker books are stitched, while the thinner books are
stapled together.

6. THE PRINT

The type used in these books is clear and pleasing. The spacing is particularly good.

7. EARLY PHRASING

In the early books the phrasing of each line of print has been carefully devised to avoid splitting meaningful, linguistic patterns, so that the child is helped in his attempts to read with an easy, comprehensible flow of language.

8. ILLUSTRATIONS

All the books are illustrated attractively in full colour. Frequently there is more than one illustration on a page and every illustration acts as a direct aid to the interpretation of the text. For example, on page 4 of Story Book 7, *Grandpa's Greenhouse*, there is a simple drawing of a man sprinkling seeds into a box. Underneath is the text:

> He sprinkles the seed on the earth
> and puts more earth on top
> and pats it.
> Then he puts on a label.
> It says 'Lettuce'.

There follows another simple illustration showing a seed box with a label displaying the word 'Lettuce'.

The result of using illustrations in this precise manner is that they never usurp the function of the text. The pictures do not lead the child's thoughts away from the text in flights of fancy, neither do they mislead the unwary. Instead, they centre his thoughts directly upon the message contained in the words and sentences.

9. RELATIONSHIP WITH WRITTEN WORK

The teacher who is looking for a scheme which combines the practice of writing with the task of learning to read will find adequate scope for this in the workbooks. And if that teacher is also looking for stories which will fire the child's imagination, both about his immediate environment and the imaginary environment created in his mind, then she will find plenty of topics on which to base the work in written and oral language.

F. OPTIMUM SITUATIONS

Situations in which *Time for Reading* would be likely to be used to the best advantage would combine some of the following features:

1. children aged five to seven years;

2. children who are of average or above average intelligence rather than of low intelligence, (although much will depend on the way in which the teacher uses the scheme as part of the total work of the class) and who come from homes of average or above average socio-economic level;

3. a teacher whose basic beliefs about reading are concerned with learning within a structured programme, rather than with teaching to a system of rules and procedures;

4. a teacher who prefers the role of consultant to that of leader, but who wishes to play a positive part rather than an indeterminate one in helping the child to learn;

5. a teacher who is not necessarily in a hurry to introduce phonic instruction, but one who does believe that it will be necessary at a particular stage;

6. a teacher who believes that learning to read involves more than merely looking at words and sentences, as it also entails using words and sentences, and writing them in a constructive manner;

7. a teacher who feels the need for some specific guidance regarding informal procedures and about all aspects of work in the classroom which impinge upon learning to read.

9 Phonic approaches

Whilst the majority of basic reading schemes published in Great Britain during the past fifteen years have followed a global approach to reading, there has developed among many teachers a desire to incorporate some form of controlled phonic instruction in their reading tuition. Three current approaches to reading have attempted to meet this need in different ways: *Royal Road Readers* (Daniels and Diack 1954), *Programmed Reading Kit* (Stott 1962) and *Fun with Phonics* (Reis 1962). Although all three approaches fall into the broad category of systematic teaching, they contrast with each other in certain respects.

The *Royal Road Readers* form a complete reading scheme which presents phonic instruction within the more traditional format of short exercises and a series of reading books. In contrast, *Programmed Reading Kit* and *Fun with Phonics* both consist almost entirely of apparatus, and each is intended as supplementary materials rather than as a complete reading scheme. Yet these two approaches centred on the use of reading apparatus differ from each other in various ways. *Programmed Reading Kit* provides a programme to guide the child by means of games and exercises through all the stages of phonic training. Its main mode of operation is through individualized activities, with children working alone, in pairs or in small groups, and with no specific provision being made for class teaching. In contrast, *Fun with Phonics* is designed especially for informal infant classes and it relies heavily upon the participation of both teacher and pupils, with the former frequently taking the role of an active leader in the games.

1. The Royal Road Readers
(Daniels, J. C. and Diack, H., 1954)

A. THE AUTHORS

I. BACKGROUND

The authors of the *Royal Road Readers* are lecturers in education at the Institute of Education in the University of Nottingham. Dr Daniels is Deputy Director of the Institute and Mr Diack is a senior lecturer. They have both been engaged for many years in research into the problems and practices of teaching children to read. The research which formed the basis for the construction of the *Royal Road Readers* is described in the following two pamphlets: *Progress in Reading* (1956) and *Progress in Reading in the Infant School* (1958).

2. BASIC BELIEFS

The authors believe in the systematic teaching of reading through a planned scheme of phonic training.

3. THE TEACHER'S MANUAL

The teacher's manual for the *Royal Road Readers*, a book of some sixty-three pages, falls into two parts. The first part contains an excellent discussion about the nature of reading and the implications this has for the teaching methods that can be used. Each of the main methods – alphabetic, phonic, look-and-say, and 'look-and-don't-say' – are examined and their deficiencies are noted. Part I ends with a description of the phonic word method used in the *Royal Road Readers*. Part II describes how the *Royal Road Readers* can be used.

If the teacher wishes to obtain the full benefit of this scheme, she would be wise to follow the plan proposed in Part II of the manual because here she will find many suggestions and ideas which will supplement the work contained in the children's books of the scheme.

The enjoyment of books in a group

*Reading and writing
go together*

'This is what I wanted!'

Unfortunately, whilst the exercises in Book One are fully explained, the exercises which appear in the reading books from Book Two onwards are not so fully described, and the teacher could miss the point of some of the exercises. In any case, she will need to examine each exercise before it is time for the children to do it.

B. MEDIUM AND METHOD

The medium used in the *Royal Road Readers* is t.o., and an analytic phonic method is employed. The authors describe their method as a 'phonic word method' and the essence of it is that the child is trained to pay attention to the details of letters within words and thereby enabled to distinguish between words of similar but not identical appearance.

C. THE SCOPE OF THE SCHEME

I. COMPLETE READING SCHEME

The *Royal Road Readers* and the *Royal Road Reading Apparatus* are intended to form a complete reading scheme. This scheme consists of ten basic books in the Main Course, twenty-two supplementary readers, four Question Time Books, a teacher's manual and a simple type of apparatus. In the main course, at the Book Two and Book Three stages, alternative books are available. These are equivalent in phonic complexity but differ in their subject matter, one being suitable for infants and the other for older pupils.

2. RANGE OF ATTAINMENTS

The reading scheme commences with the earliest stages of phonic training and introduces the complete range of phonic complexities, including polysyllabic words.

3. INTENDED PUPILS

This scheme attempts to meet the needs of both junior children who are backward in reading and infants who are expected to make normal progress. This is an extremely broad aim for a set of readers because the interests, experiences of things other than reading, and the stages of mental development of these two groups of children are so different. Teachers of infants will find a great deal of useful material in the early books, but they may need to make certain adaptations regarding the apparatus and exercises. Teachers of backward readers in junior schools will find the gradual progression through the various phonic rules and conventions and the content of the stories, with the possible exception of Books Two A and Three A, most helpful.

D. SPECIAL FEATURES OF THE SCHEME

I. ATTENTION TO MINIMAL DIFFERENCES IN WORDS

When this scheme was first published, its most striking innovation was the authors' contention that the first essential skill to be acquired in learning to read is the ability to distinguish between words which differ only in minute details. Consequently, in the *Royal Road Readers*, from the very beginning the child is called upon to distinguish between pairs of words such as 'cap' and 'cab', 'bin' and 'tin', and 'bed' and 'bud'. It was the emphasis which the authors gave to this aspect of learning to read which led them to describe their method as a 'phonic word method'.

The child is helped to make these fine distinctions by the meaningful contexts in which he meets these words. In the first instance, each individual word is related to an illustration so that the child can easily see what the word should be. Later, new words are presented in isolated sentences or in story contexts.

2. USE OF EXERCISES

A second striking feature of this scheme is the rigorous way in which phonic training begins in the first book. In Part I of Book One, in a series of exercises covering thirty pages, the child is introduced to all the simple sounds of the alphabet and certain blends, such as *st, ld, br, ft, mp, ng*. He is introduced also to simple sentences.

The first group of exercises involves matching words and phrases to simple, uncomplicated pictures, and the second group teaches the child new words and then requires him to insert letters omitted from these words.

In Part II of Book One, the children are not given so many exercises of the more mechanical type employed in Part I. Instead the exercise and practice of newly learnt words is presented in story form. This certainly adds interest to the acquisition of reading skills, but in so doing, some teachers may consider that certain of the valuable features of the exercises in Part I are lost. For example, with reference to the intensive exercise of newly learnt facts and rules, teachers may wonder why the digraphs which are introduced in Part II should not be accorded treatment similar to that used for single vowels, and also why the direct confrontation with words dissimilar only in a minor details is discontinued.

From Books Two A and Two onwards there are exercises followed by longer stories. Through these exercises runs a progression in phonic training; and many of them are exercises in comprehension. This progression is purposefully gradual so that no unreasonable effort is required from the child.

3. VOCABULARY CONTROL

Whereas it has been the practice in look-and-say schemes to control the vocabulary of graded sets of reading books by restricting both the number of new words introduced and the total number of words used in each book, the authors of the *Royal Road Readers* have decided to use another kind of vocabulary control. They are not so much concerned to limit the number of words used and introduced in each book; they prefer to limit the number of phonic complexities. Thus, although there are nearly 400 different words in Parts I and II of Book One, the phonic complexities amongst these words are very few. This means that when the child has mastered these few rules he is able to use them to interpret a large number of words. In addition to regular phonic words, forty-seven common irregular words – which the authors term 'special words' – are also introduced.

E. ADDITIONAL DETAILS

I. THE EXERCISES

a. *Their form*

Many of the exercises contained in the books involve the child in writing –
copying words or parts of words and adding letters. If the scheme is used
with infants, it would be beneficial if the teacher reconstructed some of the
exercises in the form of pieces of apparatus. Indeed, some teachers who have
used the scheme with infants suggest that the exercises at the beginning of
the scheme would be more effective and easier to use if Book One, Part I
was converted into an expendable workbook in which additional space
could be allowed for the exercises. Such an arrangement would provide
more room for very young children to write in missing letters and to lay
letter cards in the blank spaces. It would also help infants to see the results
of their interpretation of sentences if the apparatus included sentence cards
corresponding to the sentences on pages 22 to 30. The children could then
place the appropriate sentences alongside the illustrations.

b. *Instructions for use*

Most of the exercises in Book One, Part I would undoubtedly work more
effectively if they were supervised by the teacher, and all of them require
simple instructions to the child. As the form of many of the exercises is
repeated, the small amount of time spent on instructions tends to dwindle.
In Part II, and in many of the exercises in the following books, once the
teacher has initiated the exercises the children can work alone, but the
teacher has to check the child's responses at the end of the exercise.

c. *Self-checking*

The exercises are not self-checking.

d. *Relationship with written work*

Most of the exercises can involve the children in some form of writing if
the teacher wishes. On the whole this writing will take the form of copying or writing very simple answers to questions.

2. SUPPORTING APPARATUS

The scheme includes three sets of very simple apparatus, printed on durable card. Sets 1 and 2 involve matching words and pictures, and Set 3 requires the child to insert a missing letter in a word. The purpose of the apparatus is to supplement by repetition what has been learnt in the exercises of Book One Part I. As the apparatus is virtually a repetition of the exercises found in the books, few or no instructions by the teacher are necessary. The activities in which the child is engaged can only be self-checking if the child is shown how to check them against the appropriate exercise in Book One, and even this would leave room for errors.

3. THE READING BOOKS

a. Language

There are two noticeable features about the vocabulary and language used in the reading books. The first is that the style of English used in these books makes a pleasing contrast with that of many basic reading schemes, as it is precise and lucid. This is a particularly noteworthy achievement as the authors were working under the limitations imposed by a phonically controlled vocabulary.

The other point concerns the introduction of a large number of contrasting words of somewhat similar appearance, for example, 'scampering' and 'scrambling' in Book Two A. Although such pairs of words are intended to make the child pay careful attention to individual letters within words, certain teachers may question the wisdom of placing such exacting demands upon a child who is only in the early stages of competency in reading.

b. Contents of the stories

There are obvious difficulties in writing stories, within a confined series, which will suit both infants and juniors. Undoubtedly, the stories in *Royal Road Readers* are of a high quality and will be appreciated by children in the

junior school. On the other hand, the infant teacher would be well advised to think carefully about the suitability of the later books in the
scheme for infants. It is not that the subject matter is unsuitable, but it is
rather a question of whether a child in an infant class has the powers of
interpretation necessary to appreciate the meanings conveyed by innuendo
and suggestion in some of the stories.

c. Format

The covers of the main books in the scheme are of linson cloth and they
have stitched bindings, while the supplementary books are covered in
thin card and the pages are stapled together. The illustrations are clear and
uncomplicated, so that they are unlikely to mislead children.

d. The print

The typescript is clear and the publishers have avoided the temptation,
to which some submit, of radically reducing the size and spacing of the
print in the later books of the scheme.

e. Early phrasing

Unfortunately, no attempt has been made to avoid splitting meaningful
phrases, such as 'the milk can', which is printed as:

> The milkman is lifting the
> milk can.

There are numerous other examples of this.

4. THE STANDARD READING TESTS

The authors of the *Royal Road Readers* have constructed a set of twelve
reading tests which are published in a book entitled *Standard Reading Tests*
(Daniels and Diack 1958). Most of these tests are diagnostic in character
and are broadly based on the developmental plan of phonic complexities
underlying their reading scheme. The use of these tests will enable the
teacher to discover the child's weaknesses, which she can then set about
remedying by using the appropriate materials from the reading scheme.

F. OPTIMUM SITUATIONS

Situations in which the *Royal Road Readers* would be likely to be used most effectively would incorporate many of the following features:

1. junior or secondary school children who are backward in reading and who require remedial work;

2. children with a reasonably well-developed skill in spoken language;

3. a teacher who wishes to use a systematic phonic method;

4. situations in which desk-work is more appropriate than physical activity, for example with a group of backward readers working within a class of better readers;

5. situations in which the teacher does not consider it essential for reading activities to arise from general classroom activities.

2. Programmed Reading Kit
(Stott, D. H., 1962)

A. THE AUTHOR

I. BACKGROUND

The inventor of *Programmed Reading Kit*, Professor D. H. Stott, is a psychologist and educationist. He was for thirteen years a teacher of modern languages in grammar schools. He then transferred to a secondary modern school where he encountered the problem of illiteracy and became interested in teaching backward readers. His reading apparatus is the result of ten years' research into the sticking points and difficulties which children meet in learning to read. His experiments were carried out in co-operation with groups of teachers, who tested the apparatus which he devised and who made critical assessments of it.

2. BASIC BELIEFS

Stott believes in a form of systematic tuition, based upon a progressive sequence of finely graded steps in learning, and couched in an enjoyable activity.

3. TEACHER'S MANUAL

In the teacher's manual there is a concise description of the manner in which each item of apparatus can be used. The games, upon which the method so largely depends, are explained and the objectives of these games are outlined.

If, however, the teacher wishes to understand more fully the thoughts which motivated the author and the theoretical basis of the games and exercises, then it is essential to refer to chapter 3 in Stott's book, *Roads to Literacy* (1964).

B. MEDIUM AND METHOD

The medium employed in the *Programmed Reading Kit* is t.o., and an analytic phonic method is used.

C. THE SCOPE OF THE APPARATUS

1. SUPPLEMENTARY MATERIALS

The *Programmed Reading Kit* is not planned as a complete reading scheme, but as an aid to the teaching of reading. It consists of a progression of games, specially devised to give phonic training. The whole *Kit* is divided into thirty items which provide a substantial background of letter and word recognition, word manipulation, and familiarity with the phonic conventions. Sentences and very short stories are introduced in the later stages of the apparatus and Stott suggests that these may be followed by two sets of books of which he is the author: the *Day of the Week Books* (1961) and the *Micky Books* (1960). In addition, he thinks that 'any other simple Readers on phonic lines which introduce the conventions' can be introduced when the children reach Item 20 in the *Kit*.

2. RANGE OF READING ATTAINMENTS

The complete scheme covers a considerable span in reading ability, taking the 'children from a state of not even knowing what is meant by sounds to a reading level of about nine years': in fact, to a stage when they can apply the phonic rules to new words with a great deal of assurance.

3. INTENDED PUPILS

The programme of games and exercises was originally compiled for backward readers in the junior school. However, Stott sees the problem of learning to read at any age as being one that is concerned with mastering basic rules, conventions and processes of word recognition. He claims that the learning sequence, which runs through the *Kit*, can be adjusted to the learner's needs.

Miss Mary Wignall, the headmistress of an infant school, writing in Stott's book, *Roads to Literacy*, suggests that, with adjustments to some of the Items, the *Kit* can be used successfully with infants of average ability. Other teachers have also found this to be so.

D. SPECIAL FEATURES OF THE APPROACH

1. PROGRAMMED LEARNING

The whole programme is a carefully worked-out sequence of learning in which each step is a small one. Most children of all ages, beyond the pre-reading stage, could pass through these steps but it is difficult to visualize all children being enthusiastic about every Item. Hence, one would agree with Stott that the *Kit* should not stand alone. It is, as he says, 'a means of leading the child through all the mental processes needed for fluent reading'; but it cannot replace books and it cannot replace other forms of activity, such as the development of spoken language and writing, which form such an important and integral part of learning to read.

2. LEARNING THROUGH GAMES

Stott was conscious of the disadvantages apparent in the early reading books of many phonic schemes, when a stilted form of English was used in order to conform to a restricted regular phonic vocabulary. The only way to avoid this was, he decided, to rely upon exercises instead of books during the early stages. Yet he wanted to avoid exercises which did not excite the children. His solution was to construct all the exercises in the form of games, which two or more children could play while sitting at a table or desk.

3. THE TYPE OF PHONIC ATTACK

Stott begins from the basic supposition that the attempt to learn isolated individual letter sounds by means of repetitive drill is detrimental to learning. He prefers to use words and, by incorporating these words in games and exercises, he leads the child to make his own 'associations between the sounds as heard in words and the letters as seen in words'. For example, the Touch Cards and the Frame Game both require one child to name a picture which only he can see amongst other pictures, and the other child to point to the appropriate initial letter of the word spoken. In this way the child experiences letters within word sounds, which makes it easier for him to associate the printed letter with its sound.

E. ADDITIONAL DETAILS

1. PURPOSE

The title, *Programmed Reading Kit*, is an apt description of this apparatus in that it forms a series of shallow steps, through which the child must progress as he learns to read. Each step is intended to teach the child something, reinforce that knowledge and prepare him thoroughly for the next step. For example, Item 1 teaches the child the associations between letters and sounds; Item 2 reinforces these associations; Item 3 tests the child's knowledge of them; Item 4 gives further practice; and Item 5 provides a final written exercise in the initial letters of words.

2. WHAT DOES IT SUPPLEMENT?

The fact that the *Kit* is itemized, with each Item or series of Items perform-ing a specific function in the process of learning to read, enables the *Kit* (or part of it) to be used to supplement the teaching of reading that is being done through other materials and procedures, or even through another method. For example, if the teacher, using either a look-and-say or a phonic method, wishes to arrange practice for a small group of children in blending sounds to make a word, she can set them to work on the Half Moon Cards. Many teachers use the *Kit* in this way and find it extremely useful. Thus as long as the teacher is willing to note from the teacher's manual the purpose of the Items, she will be able to use part or all of the *Kit* to supplement what she is doing.

3. ORGANIZATION

The pieces of apparatus are simple and clear, and the games are not complicated. Backward children can easily and quickly understand what is required. Only a few moments need be spent on explanation by the teacher, and as many of the games recur the teacher's task is reduced even further as the child proceeds from Item to Item.

4. SERVICEABILITY

The pieces of apparatus are very easy to handle: even infants will find no difficulties in manipulating them. All the apparatus consists of pieces of card, which may appear flimsy, but which are surprisingly durable. Each item can be stored in a thick polythene sleeve and the whole *Kit* fits into a strong cardboard box which occupies very little space on the shelf of a normal classroom cupboard. Each Item is labelled with the activity or type of apparatus but this does not indicate the task that it is meant to perform.

5. SELF-CHECKING

There is a very effective system of self-checking built into some of the Items. For example, the Morris Cards in Item 2 contain pictures and matching words on one side and the appropriate initial letter on the other. The child can check the players' responses by referring to the pictures. However, certain of the Items (for example, those involving the use of the Half Moon Cards) are not self-checking and require a greater degree of participation by the teacher. Similarly, the written exercises have to be checked by the teacher; but teachers will find it encouraging to note that this is not an onerous task.

F. OPTIMUM SITUATIONS

The *Programmed Reading Kit* is likely to prove most advantageous if used in the following circumstances:

1. with children who have reached an age when they are willing to participate in, and concentrate upon, card games – probably middle and upper juniors;

2. with children of below average intelligence, who are lacking in imagination and drive, and who require remedial training in a class or in a remedial centre;

3. by a teacher who believes in systematic teaching and group work;

4. by a teacher who wishes to give small groups of children specific training in the phonic aspects of learning to read;

5. by a teacher who, believing in a look-and-say beginning and having chosen a scheme which contains no planned phonic approach, wishes to introduce some phonic instruction at particular points in the reading programme.

3. Fun with Phonics
(Reis, M., 1962)

A. THE AUTHOR

1. BACKGROUND

Mrs Muriel Reis has taught in an infant school for many years.

2. BASIC BELIEFS

The author of *Fun with Phonics* believes in a systematic approach to the teaching of reading and in the advantages that can be gained from a scheme of work which 'makes provision for the mechanics of reading to be learnt with enthusiasm, through a variety of games and activities which have a strong play element'.

3. TEACHER'S MANUAL

The teacher's manual, or handbook as Reis calls it, contains twenty-six pages and is very short when compared with other manuals. However, it describes effectively the ways in which the apparatus should be used, and it provides word lists. The manual contains a single page summary of all activities involved, which will prove a useful quick reference list for the teacher who is using the scheme for the first time.

It is a pity that the list of stages and the phonic rules that they cover, which can be found in the publisher's pamphlet, is not included in the handbook. Teachers would be wise to obtain this pamphlet to read along with the handbook.

B. MEDIUM AND METHOD

The medium employed in *Fun with Phonics* is t.o. The method is phonic, and synthetic in the first place, as the children are required to build up words from individual letter sounds. This is in contrast to the *Royal Road Readers* and *Programmed Reading Kit*, in which analytic phonic methods are used. In the later stages of *Fun with Phonics*, however, there are opportunities for the use of analytic methods and the quick sight-reading of words.

C. THE SCOPE OF THE SCHEME

I. SUPPLEMENTARY MATERIALS

Fun with Phonics is best described as a phonic course and is intended to be used alongside a reading scheme which includes books and introduces prose. This scheme consists solely of apparatus: letter, word and picture cards, post-boxes, snap cards, templates and a twirler or simple tachisto-scope.

2. RANGE OF READING ATTAINMENTS

The course begins at the earliest stage of beginning to read; there is no pre-reading stage although learning the sounds of letters may be thought to be in this category. It is not possible to give an upper limit in terms of a

reading age to which the scheme takes children, because the course con-
centrates upon word recognition; and therefore much will depend on the
reading scheme chosen to be used alongside *Fun with Phonics*. All that can
be said is that when a child has completed the course he should understand
the majority of the simpler phonic rules, although he will not have been
introduced to all the rules in the detailed manner used in *Programmed
Reading Kit* or to such an extensive range of phonic complexities as in the
Royal Road Readers.

3. INTENDED PUPILS

It is obvious from the author's background, her handbook, and from the
type of games and exercises introduced, that this course is intended for
infants, although parts of it could be adapted for use with older pupils.
The nature of the work demands an informal attitude to the movement of
children within the classroom.

D. SPECIAL FEATURES

1. GROUP AND INDIVIDUAL ACTIVITIES

Fun with Phonics attempts to meet the needs of the teacher in a teacher-
orientated situation, as opposed to the individual learning situation of the
Programmed Reading Kit. The games are based upon the principle of group
co-operation, in which the children come together in groups, actively and
physically participating in a teacher-learner situation. For example, the
teacher may be conducting a period of word recognition. She places flash
cards in the twirler, exposes them to the group of children who have to
act upon the message they get from the words, such as 'run', 'hop', or
'sit'. The whole scheme is based upon a very simple plan. The teacher
introduces each stage and she employs class games to illustrate her teaching. This is followed at every stage by independent practice in the work
that has just been learnt.

2. MOVEMENT

A basic idea behind the games is that movement is a necessary part of
learning to read. This involves the movement of children to perform such

meaningful and enjoyable tasks as hiding, posting letters and words, and responding to a written instruction; the movement of letters, whether hung round a child's neck or on the desk in front of the child, to form words – a type of physical blending of visual symbols accompanied by their appropriate sounds; and singing which controls the movement of the children.

Here again there is a strong contrast between the *Programmed Reading Kit*, where the games are played with cards at a table, and *Fun with Phonics*, where children move about the classroom or in the case of some games, the playground, taking their cards with them.

3. LETTERS BEFORE WORDS

The first stage of *Fun With Phonics* consists of singing games in which the children learn the sound of each letter in the alphabet without seeing that letter in a written word. For example, each child has a letter written on a card which is hung round his neck. To the tune, 'London Bridge is Broken Down', the class sing:

> Run off little letter 'O',
> Letter 'O', letter 'O',
> Run off little letter 'O',
> My Fair Lady.

This is followed by 'Come back, little letter "O" ', and so on. The only indication the child has that this letter sound is connected with a word is through the picture, on the back of his card, which illustrates an object whose name begins with that letter.

In connection with this practice of learning the sounds of separate letters, it should be noted that many linguists and teachers find it difficult to produce accurately the correct sound of a letter isolated from a complete word sound and, accordingly, the practice of introducing letters before words has been dropped by writers of certain phonic schemes; for example Daniels and Diack in the *Royal Road Readers*. Stott, although he introduces the child to letter sounds in the first stages of his *Programmed Reading Kit*, does it by showing the child words whose initial letter is the one to be learnt.

E. ADDITIONAL DETAILS

I. PURPOSE

Fun with Phonics is a complete course of phonic instruction. Each stage within that course consists of two parts:
a. the Class Games in which the teacher introduces the subject matter to be learnt;
b. the Independent Activities, which give practice in the work taken by the teacher in the preceding Class Games.

2. WHAT DOES IT SUPPLEMENT?

The phonic training provided by the apparatus and games of *Fun with Phonics* would prove a useful supplement to any look-and-say scheme, but particularly to one devoid of phonic work.

4. SERVICEABILITY

The apparatus has been planned by a teacher of infants and it is easily handled by young children. Each piece of apparatus is made of thin card which is more durable than appears to be the case at first sight. This card can be strengthened, if it is thought necessary, by covering it with adhesive transparent polythene. The post-boxes, which are also made of card, should not be placed on radiators or anywhere else where they would be exposed to heat, otherwise they may curl.

5. INSTRUCTIONS FOR USE

The Class Activities and some of the Independent Activities in which children are moving about and doing things, presuppose a fair degree of competence on the teacher's part in both class control and classroom organization. However, the games and activities are not complicated and do not require a lot of explanation. Even young children can easily understand what has to be done.

The pleasures of reading and listening

The usefulness of reading

6. SELF-CHECKING

The child cannot check his own work on the apparatus, but by the use of
eight distinct colours for the letter and word cards, the teacher can check
each child's response at a glance, so that she can help any child in difficulties.

7. ONE DISTINCTIVE INNOVATION

The twirler is an interesting innovation for general use in schools. It is a
wooden box-like construction, which revolves half a turn on a horizontal
axis. A flash card containing a word is placed in the twirler, and by simply
revolving the box, the teacher can flash words at a uniform rate. More
sophisticated types of tachistoscope have been used by researchers for
many years but teachers have rarely used this type of equipment. Reis
makes three points about the use of the twirler: it can be used for the
quick recognition of words; it can be used as a pacer to increase the speed
of recognition and to increase confidence; and the children can use it as
a face-saver, whereby those who fail to read a word can blame the twirler
for going too quickly, rather than blame themselves for not knowing a
word. The third point is particularly interesting and could well have
important implications for infants and for older backward readers, both
of whom depend so greatly upon a growing self-confidence to help them
along.

F. OPTIMUM SITUATIONS

The fact that *Fun with Phonics* is a course in the phonic rules of English, and
is restricted to letters and isolated words, means that it can only be used as
part of a reading programme – books and English prose being also
required. Therefore it is likely to be used to the best advantage under a
combination of the following circumstances:

1. with children aged five to seven years;
2. in classrooms where there is room for the children to move about;
3. with a teacher who is prepared to initiate learning of the phonic rules,

participate in some of the activities, and control the movement of children about the classroom;

4. with a teacher who is sympathetic towards an informal classroom atmosphere, but one who nevertheless believes in the necessity for systematic teaching;

5. with a teacher who is willing to use a considerable amount of apparatus in the classroom;

6. with a teacher who is looking for a course of systematic phonic instruction, unattached to any set of reading books, so that she is free to select those books which she considers most appropriate.

10 Approaches introducing different media

Three new approaches to beginning reading, involving the use of new media, are examined in this chapter: *Words in Colour* (Gattegno 1962), *Colour Story Reading* (Jones 1967) and *i.t.a.* (Pitman 1959). Although these approaches have certain features in common, they have even more features which distinguish them from each other.

The three inventors share two common attributes. First, their interest in beginning reading is centred on the nature of the task. They all believe that the irregularities of t.o. are responsible for many of the problems encountered in learning to read, and it was their endeavours to mitigate or abolish the inconsistencies of t.o. which led them to devise these three different media. Secondly, it is interesting to note that, at the time when he first turned his attention to the problem of devising a regularized medium, none of the inventors of these approaches appears to have had previous experience of teaching the early stages of reading to young children.

The most common features of these three approaches are as follows. First, as each is based on a medium other than t.o., each requires specially printed reading materials. Secondly, in each case, teachers who are going to use the new medium must do a certain amount of preliminary reading and other preparation in order to familiarize themselves with the new code. This contrasts with the use of approaches based on t.o. where, although it is desirable that teachers should study the teacher's manuals before using the schemes, some teachers do manage to use them more or less effectively without undertaking this preliminary study.

In most other respects the three approaches contrast with each other, in ways which will become clear as each is examined in detail. A brief summary of the main differences between these approaches is given at the end of this chapter.

1. Words in Colour
(Gattegno, C., 1962)

A. THE AUTHOR

I. BACKGROUND

Dr Caleb Gattegno, the inventor of *Words in Colour*, a remarkable man who has shown great originality in simplifying and structuring learning processes, was born in Belgium. His early experiences as a teacher led to publications relating to the teaching of art, geography, biology, music and mathematics. Later he was a lecturer in mathematics and education at the University of London. His endeavours to improve the teaching of mathematics at both primary and secondary levels led to the publication of *Numbers in Colour* (1954), relating to the use of the Cuisenaire rods, with which so many teachers are now familiar.

As UNESCO's consultant for International Education, he worked in Ethiopia devising ways of teaching adult illiterates to read their official language, Amharic. He states himself that when he first turned his attention to the teaching of reading and writing in 1957 he was no expert and had never taught very young children to read or write any language. He soon realized that the techniques he had developed in Ethiopia could be adapted to teaching the English language. His experiments with five- and six-year-olds in Canada, in the United States and in Great Britain convinced him that this was so, and led to the production of *Words in Colour* in English. This approach has since been extended to certain other languages.

2. BASIC BELIEFS

Gattegno views learning to read and write primarily in terms of mastery of a code, a process which he believes can be simplified and accelerated by a finely-graded systematic plan of tuition. To further this end he lays down explicit stages of progression and definite lesson plans. Accordingly, although he emphasizes the importance of the learner and the necessity for delegating responsibility to him, his beliefs, as far as the terms employed in this book are concerned, must undoubtedly be classified as falling into the category of 'systematic teaching'.

3. TEACHER'S MANUAL

Gattegno has provided ample evidence of his beliefs about reading, the rationale underlying his approach, descriptions of the materials, meticulous instructions as to how the materials should be used, and comments on the roles of both teacher and pupil in *Words in Colour – Background and Principles* and its companion book *Words in Colour – Teacher's Guide.** The former gives a clear account of Gattegno's views on the English language and the relationship between speech, handwriting and reading, as well as an outline and summary of his approach. It also includes lists of the words shown on his charts (see examples opposite pages 152 and 153 of this book). The latter book includes descriptions of the materials, detailed plans of development for lessons and general remarks regarding the teacher's attitude to this approach, the use of dynamic imagery in learning to read and class management.

Although throughout this book the necessity has been emphasized for any teacher appraising a new approach to reading to begin by examining the teacher's manual, in the case of *Words in Colour* it is absolutely essential that this should be done. The two teacher's books mentioned should preferably be read before the reading materials are examined. This is important because the appearance of the reading materials themselves is, at first glance, unlikely to attract most teachers, particularly those in charge of infants. Only by first reading the author's explanation of his ideas – ideas which are very different from those of the authors of many reading approaches but which nevertheless merit serious consideration – will the teacher be in a position to make a fair assessment of the total plan, including the reading materials.

A number of publications relating to teachers' experiences with *Words in Colour* are also available and certain of these are included in 'Suggestions for Further Reading' at the end of this chapter.

---

* As this book was going to press, Gattegno's latest book was published: Gattegno, C. (1969) *Reading with Words in Colour: A Scientific Study of the Problems of Reading*. Reading, Berks: Educational Explorers.

B.   MEDIUM AND METHOD

The medium employed in *Words in Colour* represents a signalling system in the form of a complete colour code. It is, moreover, an absolutely consistent colour code in which each colour represents one sound and one sound only: it incorporates neither deviations, alternatives nor ambiguities.

The method used is a synthetic phonic one, in which sounds are combined to form words.

C.   THE SCOPE OF THE APPROACH

I.   A COMPLETE SCHEME

Words in Colour has been planned as a complete course of beginning reading tuition. Furthermore, it is essential to note that it also represents a total approach to reading instruction, in that the author assumes that no other reading materials will be used until the child has mastered the whole reading programme. The materials in this scheme – wall charts, basic books, worksheets and one set of cards – represent all that the author considers necessary. In practice, it should prove possible for children who have worked through a proportion of the scheme to read simple supplementary books, particularly those phonically based, although no doubt Gattegno would frown on this practice.

2.   RANGE OF READING ATTAINMENTS

Words in Colour is designed for the absolute beginner, and the work is so structured as to lead the learner eventually to fluent reading and mastery of the entire 274 sound-symbol relationships which Gattegno identifies in the English language. A child who has fully mastered this entire course, although he may not have read many books outside the scheme, should be in a position to attempt to read almost anything he wishes. His reading ability might be about that of an average nine-year-old, but it could well be much higher, particularly if it were measured on a test such as Schonell's *Graded Word Reading Test* (1945) which depends to a large extent on the correct pronunciation of unconnected words.

3. INTENDED PUPILS

Gattegno's approach to learning to read, having first been developed with adults and later used with both infants and older pupils who were backward in reading, is intended for children and adults of all ages who have not begun to learn to read or who have tried with other approaches and failed.

D. OUTLINE OF THE APPROACH

A teacher deciding to use *Words in Colour* is doing much more than selecting a new medium: she is choosing a very definite approach to reading in which medium, materials, method and procedures are all strictly regulated. A regular medium in the form of a colour code is utilized, within a limited range of materials; a phonic method is employed, and the formal teaching procedures which are advocated must inevitably determine many of the general classroom procedures. It seems fairly certain that the precise instructions given for teaching methods are equally as important, if not more important, than the colour code itself. Thus the use of *Words in Colour* will necessarily limit the teacher in certain respects, while providing her with detailed rules and guidance for work within the defined limits.

I. THE MEDIUM – AN ABSOLUTELY REGULAR COLOUR CODE

Gattegno's aim was to make English into a phonetic language without altering the traditional spelling of English words. He has done this by using colours to indicate sounds; the same colour always being used for the same sound, whatever the spelling. For example, the 'ee' sound in the word 'he' is represented by a bright red letter 'e'. The same bright red is used for the letters which represent the sound 'ee' in every other English word, for example the following words (the relevant letters being printed in italics here merely for clarity):

> s*ee*, k*e*y, dr*ea*m, p*eo*ple, bel*ie*ve, rec*ei*ve, pol*i*cemen, qu*ay*side, and s*e*cret

Conversely, if a letter or combination of letters, for example, 'ea' represents different sounds in different words such as 'eat', 'heavy', 'great', 'bear' and 'earl', the relevant letters are printed in different colours in each word.

Gattegno has identified forty-seven sounds in the English language and assigned to each a particular colour, with the result that many different shades and tints of basic colours are used; in addition, certain letters are two-toned, with the top half of a letter being one colour and the lower half another colour. The result is a complete colour code, the colour signals indicating to the learner exactly how to pronounce every word. It is also an absolutely consistent colour code in which the signals are always true. There are no deviations from the invariable rule that a letter or group of letters printed in a certain colour represent a particular sound.

The coloured letters are employed only on the wall charts and by the teacher when she writes on the blackboard. In fact, the use of colour is intended only for the introduction, in general stages, of the various sounds, and for later visual imagery. It also helps children who want to check or refer back to certain sounds on the wall charts. When the children write letters and words they use only one colour, and their own basic books and worksheets are printed in black.

2. THE READING MATERIALS

The materials in this reading course are as follows.

a. First, there is a set of twenty-one wall charts, printed in colour, on black backgrounds, in an italic type similar to cursive script. (Examples of *Words in Colour* wall charts are shown opposite this page.) The first chart shows various combinations of the five vowels, while the remaining twenty charts consist entirely of separate words, unrelated as far as meaning is concerned but related in respect of spelling and sound patterns, and graded according to complexity. The charts are designed for instruction purposes, the teacher being expected to point to words and lead the children through a series of oral exercises or games. They are also meant to be displayed on the walls for reference.

b. There are three basic children's books related to the twenty-one coloured wall charts. They contain neither illustrations nor continuous

Four Word Charts from *Words in Colour*

```
a   a   aa   aaa
u   u   uu   uuu
au  ua  uau  aua
 i   i   ii   iii
au  ua  uu   au
 e   e   ee   eee
ae  eua  eau
 o   o   oo   ooo
aaeeoo  ieoi
oaa  aoie  oou
```

```
a    it   pet
pot  at   it   u
ap   tip  o
ep   pup  po   o
a    us   is
sa   sit  se
so   sep  oss
sos  sess  s a
sa   ss   es   es
```

```
let   lad   sell   tell
lots  smell  smell  sla
Ist   slit   doll   dull
mill  ill   until  ill
lend  lent  land   less
unless  filthy  funny
wet   wit   with
swim  was   will
sunset  slept
```

```
ant   wins   thus   ra
ran   red   fur   stir
my   sister   wild   mind
res   kid   kit   kill
neck  milk   skill   silk
kiss   ile   mile
skip   sick   line   fine
truck  track  struck
run   rust   strike
```

See also the last page of this colour section for four
further charts from *Words in Colour*.
The actual size of each chart is $22\frac{1}{4}''$ x 16″.

Blue letter z said, "I can help to make lazy zebra."

Red letter x said, "I can help to make fox."

The blue letters qu help to make quick squirrel.

Book 3 (actual size)

aeroplane cowboy legs round than

all cross loud said they

are Ernest make saw to

bad fireworks more shop took

balloon four noise sky up

blue fox of smoke was

boys good or some were

can I party square what

car into pilot squirrel zebra

cloud lazy quick tent zoo

Four Word Charts from *Words in Colour*

Chart 1

sold thirty no gone
dirty off hundred
seven a ril usable five
give tiger thanks
ho se thirsty hungry
dog gold bankrupt
front firm duty
loss so horse robe
big gun bigger

Chart 2

sho sh sh ina
ur n shall
shred chigan cken
w sh err for or
nor chorus ild
ldren ho el f
shu annel
shell sho done doe
s goe ll have

Chart 3

elephant physics
photograph foot be
see sleep feet been
why where when
who whom whose
these between you
youth our your sou
hour young sing
house courageous

Chart 4

eye day ay
high thigh nigh
ey sa urday
gray greyhound
mon hon rey
rayers wood would
should cool feld
aged finished
conceived conce

reading matter. Book 1 deals solely with five vowels and three consonants which are combined into nonsense words and simple regular words. A few sentences such as 'pat is up' and 'pat spits' appear on the final page, without punctuation marks. Books 2 and 3 introduce further consonants, digraphs and combinations of letters to complete the total number of 274 sign-sound relationships introduced on the wall charts. The text of these three books consists of single letters, groups of letters, discrete words and unrelated sentences such as the following two from Book 3:

- the circus visits the city twice every twelve
  months

and – a diaphragm closes the opening in front of
  photographic lenses.

c. A series of fourteen worksheets complements the work done with the twenty-one charts and the basic books. These worksheets consist mainly of exercises based on words which have been taught. In games of transformation children learn to juggle the letters within words, add new letters and so on in operations which Gattegno describes as substitutions, inversions, additions, and insertions – operations with which the children have become familiar while working with the teacher on the charts. For example, the word 'pat' can be changed into the word 'steps' by the following processes:

pat	– tap	(inversion)
tap	– top	(substitution)
top	– tops	(addition)
tops	– stops	(addition)
stops	– steps	(substitution)

In these worksheets the children are also asked to make up sentences from the words found on various charts or from other words they know. The final two worksheets differ from the preceding twelve as they are mainly concerned with literary matters instead of linguistic matters.

d. Eight additional coloured wall charts, named 'The English Fidel', are intended to be kept on permanent display in the classroom. The different ways of spelling the sounds found in English words are presented in columns on this Fidel, in the same colours as in the twenty-one word charts. For example, on the first chart the following list is printed in magenta: 'i', 'y', 'ey', 'u', 'o', 'ie', 'ia', 'a', 'ay', 'e', 'ai', 'ei', 'ui', while on the second chart the following list is printed in yellow: 'I', 'i', 'y', 'igh', 'eye', 'ye', 'eigh', 'is', 'ais'. The first list illustrates thirteen ways of spelling the short sound of 'i', while the second list indicates ten different ways of spelling the long sound of 'i'. This Fidel forms an interesting, and even intriguing presentation of the 274 ways of spelling the forty-seven different English sounds distinguished by Gattegno. It lends itself to being used in various teaching ways and as a useful reference list.

e.   A pupil's *Word Building Book* of sixteen pages consists solely of lists of groups of letters representing the sounds shown on the Fidel. These sounds are introduced in stages, page 1 showing nothing but eight spaced-out letters, while the final pages comprise the complete Fidel.

f.   A pupil's *Book of Stories* is the only continuous reading material provided in *Words of Colour*. Its ninety-nine pages contain forty stories describing events in the daily life of a typical family, illustrated by eleven black line drawings. Most of the book is printed in the same typeface as the wall charts, the earliest stories being without capital letters and punctuation marks. Punctuation marks are introduced gradually through-out the book and the final thirteen pages appear in a normal roman print, using capital letters as well as punctuation marks.

g.   A pack of 'Word Cards' is available for children to use later in the course for a variety of word games. Some 1,400 words are printed in roman type on cards of different colours. The colour of each card denotes a part of speech, so that nouns appear on green cards, verbs on pink cards and so on. Children are expected to assemble individual cards to form sentences, and it is suggested that by doing so they will become aware of the grammatical function of words.

h.   Finally, a set of fourteen coloured blackboard chalks is available for *Words in Colour*, and a film strip of twenty-nine frames, one for each of the wall charts.

3.   THE RATIONALE UNDERLYING THE APPROACH

Any description of *Words in Colour* would prove totally inadequate if it were restricted to a few notes on the medium and the materials without reference to the rationale underlying this approach. *Words in Colour* probably represents the most complicated approach to be considered in this book, and it is undoubtedly the one which teachers will experience most difficulty in evaluating fairly. The reasons for this are to be found partly in the appearance of the reading materials and the suggested procedures, neither of which is likely to hold initial appeal for many British primary teachers; and partly in the fact that not only are the author's ideas somewhat revolutionary as far as British infant education is concerned, but also because he uses terms which are not generally employed in this context. Indeed, Gattegno's own description of the rationale underlying his approach is not easy to understand, and the authors of this book have experienced a certain amount of difficulty in abstracting the main points and attempting to couch them in simple language. In so doing, it may be that they have failed to do justice to Gattegno's theory. Nevertheless, a brief attempt to abstract some of the major points of the rationale behind this approach may help clarify certain features about which teachers might harbour doubts.

Gattegno starts from the fact that children have already acquired a spoken language and that this must be used for teaching writing and reading. The sounds of speech must be transcribed through an adequate code into a set of written signs. Thus writing must precede reading. With *Words in Colour*, from the beginning the child learns to write the appropriate symbols for the sounds of speech.

Gattegno considers it essential that teaching should develop 'towards automatic assimilation as soon as possible'. By this he means that, 'Delegation of responsibility to the learner, at once, and all the time, is essential.' In practice this involves letting children discover the relationship between sounds and symbols for themselves, and by creating situations where children are forced to do the thinking without clues from their teachers. The teacher must only give the learner the clues which he cannot discover for himself. After that the learner must do the work. This process Gattegno describes as dynamic. He says, '... the most distinctive characteristic of our approach was not to be found so much in the use of colour to make a language quasi-phonetic, but in the fact that we make use of the dynamic properties of the mind'.

Although a proportion of teachers may initially regard *Words in Colour* as leaning heavily on drill, memory work and repetition, Gattegno strongly refutes this. He says, 'If we insist on the use of memory, that is to say, on drill and repetition, we hamper our children and create memory tracks where dynamic mental structures are needed.' He goes on to emphasize, 'We shall resort to memory as little as possible.' In his view, a look-and-say approach is a static one because it leans so heavily on memorization, whereas *Words in Colour* is dynamic because the child is constantly being required to combine and re-combine letters, syllables and words in continually changing patterns.

Gattegno's idea of the teacher's role also forms a central point of his philosophy. He states, 'Finally, since it is the children who must learn there is no point in the teacher making corrections for the child who makes mistakes; rather must she study the mistakes and organize the learning situation so that the mistakes are discovered by the children themselves, and so that they learn to avoid them.' He goes on, 'In our lessons, we find that we soon reach the point where our role is simply to analyse the steps to be taken by the children, and though it may look as if we are not teaching at all, we are, in fact, extremely active, finding out what to do to overcome obstacles which the children are meeting in what we are doing. We regard this as truly creative teaching and as such, it is far more rewarding than teaching which involves drill and memory work.'

E. SPECIAL FEATURES OF THIS APPROACH

Most of the special features of this approach have already been described fairly fully in the preceding pages. Accordingly, they need only be listed quite briefly here.

1. *Words in Colour* employs a complete and absolutely consistent colour code which tells the child exactly how to pronounce any word written in the code.

2. It consists of a limited range of reading materials and teachers are discouraged from introducing other materials. Thus it represents a total approach to beginning reading.

3. Ways of introducing the code and utilizing the materials are laid down in detail. The suggested methods and procedures, which are quite formal, are as important a part of the approach as does the colour code itself.

4. It extends beyond the stage usually referred to as beginning reading, to include every sound-symbol relationship within the English language.

F.   ADDITIONAL FEATURES OF THE APPROACH

1.   AN ACCELERATED APPROACH

Words in Colour is an accelerated approach to mastery of the mechanics of reading. For example, it is suggested that thirty-five to forty hours' instruction is the time that an average six-year-old would require to complete the course. This is achieved by 'lessons' of a very high degree of concentration in which every minute to be spent by both teacher and learner is directed towards progressive mastery of essential features of the code consisting of sound-symbol relationships.

2.   SUCCESS ASSURED

The learning situations for the child are systematically structured in very small stages so that failure is almost impossible. Each small, successful step in the learning process leads to the next step and, if any difficulty is experienced, the child is guided to the preceding known steps in such a way as to induce him to assimilate the new step with understanding. Each new step is explored in every direction.

3.   MOTIVATION

There is no extraneous motivation in the books or on the wall charts, such as coloured illustrations depicting interesting characters and incidents, nor can the teacher use a story approach to stimulate or increase a child's interest in reading. Gattegno assumes that once the child has made a start with his approach, the inevitable success and widening possibilities of exploring letters, sounds and words will have an exhilarating effect leading to increased motivation.

This is in direct contrast to current practice in many progressive infant schools where the child's motivation to begin to read and write springs from the interests and activities of the class, and all reading and writing continues to form an integral part of the life of the class. Gattegno's approach of regarding learning to read and write as a separate and concentrated activity, almost extraneous to the other activities of the class, is clearly quite different.

4. CLASS OR GROUP INSTRUCTION

This approach starts with class or group instruction and later extends to smaller groups or individual work according to individual needs and rates of progress. The 'games' which it is suggested that children might play all invoke mental rather than physical activities and they are usually teacher-directed. Most of them, apart from the assembly of individual word cards to make sentences, are centred on the wall charts and work-sheets or they entail children writing letters and words.

5. BLENDING SOUNDS

It is claimed that the difficulty of blending sounds, so often encountered by young children, is overcome by introducing consonants with vowels rather than singly. In fact, the letters are not at first named, either by reference to the names of letters or by the more common practice of naming the letters by the sounds they represent. Letters are referred to at first only by their colours: for example, 'p' is 'the brown one' and 't' is 'the purple one'.

6. VISUAL DICTATION

What Gattegno calls 'visual dictation' forms an important element in this approach. The teacher or child uses a pointer to indicate a succession of sounds or words on the blackboard or a wall chart. The children watch the movement of the pointer and either write or speak the relevant sounds, words or sentences. As listening, speaking, reading and writing advance together, the result is that both auditory and visual discrimination are developed to a high degree, and flexibility in combining and re-combining sounds and symbols is achieved. Paying attention to individual letters and their order in words becomes automatic.

7. SPELLING

The use of visual dictation and reference to the Fidel charts cannot fail to have a beneficial effect on a child's ability to spell. He will soon become acquainted with the range of possible spellings for one sound. Experience will increase his ability to select the appropriate spelling from this range of possibilities. His spelling ability will thus increase automatically along-side his growing mastery of reading skill.

8. WRITING

The writing which the child can do, and is encouraged to do, from the beginning, arises from his exploration of the possibilities of combining letters and words in a variety of ways. But the colour code employed in *Words in Colour* is not a reversible code. Its primary purpose is to simplify 'decoding' rather than 'encoding': that is, reading rather than writing. It cannot act as an unrestricted writing code, enabling the child to write any word he wishes from an early stage in the course. Gattegno states, 'This approach does not make it possible for children to write about their own experiences from the beginning.' He goes on, 'On the other hand, their learning is so much accelerated in this approach that it only means postponing this sort of creative writing for a few weeks.' Even if one is rather dubious about the phrase 'a few weeks', it seems clear that a child who has been trained by visual dictation and use of the Fidel chart will soon be able to make praiseworthy attempts to write down many of the words he wishes to write.

Gattegno also suggests how cursive writing may be taught alongside reading beginning with 'a' and, by various amendments, changing it into the other vowels.

9. WALL SPACE

The wall charts each measure 22 inches by 16 inches (about 560 mm by 400 mm), and many of these are meant to be on permanent display. They are likely to monopolize much of the available wall space in a classroom and this may create problems in a modern classroom in which there is more window space than wall space.

G. OPTIMUM SITUATIONS

Words in Colour is likely to prove effective as a means of mastering the skills of reading and writing in a wide variety of situations. It may well be considered by many teachers to be more suitable for older pupils than for younger ones, although it has been used successfully with infants. It would be equally appropriate for use with pupils of all levels of ability and of different home backgrounds. Optimum situations for using *Words in Colour* would seem to include the following factors:

1. non-English speaking people who wish to learn the language;

2. adult English-speaking illiterates;

3. retarded or backward older pupils in primary or secondary schools, and pupils in educationally sub-normal special schools, who have failed to learn to read by other approaches or whose reading progress is limited due to their lack of knowledge of the phonic principles underlying the English language;

4. remedial work with individuals or with small groups of children, in remedial centres and child guidance clinics;

5. with older infants who have begun to learn to read by a look-and-say approach and whose teacher considers they need some systematic phonic training to aid reading and spelling;

6. with young infants who are beginning to learn to read, if the following conditions hold good:

    a. the teacher is concerned about the difficulties of the task of learning to read and is looking for a systematic way of mastering the code,

    b. the teacher does not consider it essential that learning to read and write should be integrated, from the earliest stages, with all the activities of school, home and environment,

    c. the teacher looks for early, speedy, mastery of reading skill and is prepared to have this work isolated for a while from the other activities of an infant class,

    d. the teacher is willing to adopt the role of instructor for part of her time,

    e. the teacher is not averse to a certain amount of formality in classroom procedures.

SUGGESTIONS FOR FURTHER READING

(Referring to *Words in Colour*)

The following three books by Gattegno supply the rationale underlying this approach to reading, as well as detailed guidance on teaching methods and procedures. The first two books have been quoted fairly extensively in this chapter; the third one was published as this book was being completed.

GATTEGNO, C. (1962b) *Words in Colour: Background and Principles.* Reading, Berks: Educational Explorers.

GATTEGNO, C. (1962c) *Words in Colour:* Teacher's Guide. Reading, Berks Educational Explorers.

GATTEGNO, C. (1969) *Reading with Words in Colour: A Scientific Study of the Problems of Reading.* Reading, Berks: Educational Explorers.

The following two shorter and very clear accounts of *Words in Colour*, written by a local authority adviser for primary schools, are likely to provide the reader with a simpler initial description of this approach than the foregoing books by the author:

DEAN, J. (1966) 'Words in Colour.' In DOWNING, J. A. (ed.) *The First International Reading Symposium, Oxford 1964*, pp. 74–91. London: Cassell.

DEAN, J. (1967) 'Second report on Words in Colour.' In DOWNING, J. A. and BROWN, A. L. (eds.) *The Second International Reading Symposium*, pp. 169–178. London: Cassell.

Another short account of *Words in Colour* being used in a local education authority, which includes test results from four different groups of pupils, is given in:

LEE, T. (1967) 'Writing the talking: an appraisal of Words in Colour.' In BROWN, A. L. (ed.) *Reading: Current Research and Practice*, Vol. I, 1966–67, pp. 59–67. Edinburgh: Chambers.

Each of the following two books presents an interesting case study of the use of *Words in Colour* with a backward boy:

MURPHY, Sister Mary Leonore (1968a) *Douglas Can't Read*. Reading, Berks: Educational Explorers.

MURPHY, Sister Mary Leonore (1968b) *Barnaby: The Struggle of a Word-blind Boy*. Reading, Berks: Educational Explorers.

2. Colour Story Reading
(Jones, J. K., 1967b)

A. THE AUTHOR

I. BACKGROUND

Very little information has been published regarding Mr J. Kenneth Jones, other than that between 1959 and 1967 he carried out experiments with *Colour Story Reading* in primary schools, special schools for E.S.N. children and in remedial situations. He received a grant from the Department of Education and Science to carry out an investigation into the value of his phonetic colour code in early reading, and the research project was carried out in association with the Reading Research Unit of the University of London Institute of Education. The results were published in *Colour Story Reading: A Research Report* (Jones 1967a). As the publishers of *Colour Story Reading* refrain from mentioning the author's teaching experience, one can only assume that he has never been a teacher.

2. BASIC BELIEFS

The author of *Colour Story Reading* states that one of his main aims was 'to create a purposeful series of learning situations which will help children to acquire basic reading skills for themselves.' In doing so, he says that he has endeavoured to give 'complete consistency and reliability to the phonetic clues which already exist in black print . . .'. These two purposes clearly place his basic beliefs as falling into the category of systematic tuition.

3. THE TEACHER'S MANUAL

In the ninety-page teacher's manual for *Colour Story Reading*, Jones states his purposes in devising this particular code and lists the advantages of using colour to help young children to learn to read. Full details of the code itself are set out in such a way as to help the teacher to familiarize herself with it. The coloured charts shown at the end of the book and the seven-page list of words to help in learning the usage of the colour symbol code are particularly helpful in this respect. However, it should be mentioned that a teacher who merely glances at these pages may mistakenly assume that the code is such as to regularize all words, and also that the total number of words used in the children's books is larger than is actually the case.

The reading materials are described in the manual and suggestions and recommendations made for their use. These recommendations contrast with the precise instructions laid down in *Words in Colour* and give support to Jones' claim that his approach is flexible. The author's suggestions of suitable activities and games are useful and demonstrate that he is familiar with the procedures in force in infant classes. Comments are made on the relationship between *Colour Story Reading* and children's writing and spelling, as well as on special problems which may arise. The manual concludes with a section on background research, set out in simple terms.

B. THE MEDIUM AND METHOD

The medium employed in *Colour Story Reading* is a signalling system in the form of a colour code. Jones clearly considers it as a complete colour code but the authors of this book would not agree that it is a 'complete' code in the same sense as Gattegno's code. For reasons which are set out later, it appears preferable to consider it as a 'partial' code.

Regarding the method, Jones states that *Colour Story Reading* combines 'the advantages of "look-and-say" with "phonetic" assistance as aids to interpreting the sounds of written speech.' Yet the fact that the child's first book commences with individual sounds, proceeds to regular words and later to simple sentences – all employing a limited range of sounds and letters – means that, with reference to the terms employed in this book, the method must be classified as phonic. It contains elements of both analytic and synthetic phonic methods, but the major emphasis is on an analytic approach, with the child being introduced to words mainly in sentences and stories, while the colour code helps him to analyse the words.

C. THE SCOPE OF THE APPROACH

I. A COMPLETE SCHEME OR NOT?

A teacher reading through the teacher's manual for *Colour Story Reading* might be forgiven if she found herself unable to decide whether it was intended as a complete reading scheme or as supporting materials. The author does not make this point clear in the manual, although he gives a clue that it might be used alongside other reading materials when he says, '*Colour Story Reading* is in no way incompatible with black print. In fact, the more children read in colour, the greater will be their enthusiasm and skill in tackling black print.' In his research report, Jones (1967a) does mention schools which used *Colour Story Reading* for only half an hour a week and others which employed it as the main reading course in the early stages. Moreover, the results he quotes show that children in those schools which relied most heavily on *Colour Story Reading* scored more highly on reading tests than children in schools which used it sparingly.

Teachers examining the reading materials for this approach would be likely to suspect that it could not be termed a 'complete reading scheme' in the same sense as are some of the other approaches considered – for example, the three look-and-say schemes examined in chapter 8 or *Words in Colour*. The materials consist of a teacher's manual, a book of stories to be read to the children and records of the same stories, one wall chart and three short children's reading books which employ only a limited number of different words (see examples on pages 2 and 3 of colour inset between pages 152–3). Supplementary story books, worksheets, flash cards and so on are not available. It is thus probably best to consider *Colour Story Reading* as a short introductory course for beginning reading, which may or may not be supplemented by extraneous supportive materials in black print or may be used alongside a t.o. reading scheme, at the teacher's discretion. It would, however, have been preferable to have had this stated clearly in the teacher's manual. Teachers would also have found it more helpful if they had been given some specific guidance on whether better results could be expected by using only *Colour Story Reading* in the initial stages and, if reading materials in black print are to be used simultaneously, what they should be and how and at what stage they might best be introduced.

2. RANGE OF READING ATTAINMENTS

Although this approach commences at the earliest stage of formal reading tuition, it is difficult to fix an upper level of attainment which one might expect the average child who has completed the course to achieve. (The same is true of all phonic schemes and approaches which employ regularized media along phonic lines.) It clearly does not aim to reach the level of phonic complexities covered in the *Royal Road Readers, Programmed Reading Kit* or *Words in Colour*. Neither does it aim to have introduced children to such a variety of words as, for example, *Queensway Reading*. (Indeed, the total number of different words used in the three children's books of *Colour Story Reading* is only 121, although a teacher who has followed the author's suggestions for supplementary work will have introduced additional regular words.) All that can be suggested about the upper level of attainment is that use of the teacher's book of stories and the children's three books alone, without supplementary work, might take children to the level of reading ability of average children of perhaps six or six-and-a-half years, and that a good deal of supplementary work and additional reading materials would be required before children attained the standard usually associated with the upper end of most infant courses.

3. INTENDED PUPILS

Jones says that the stories which the teacher reads to the children were written with five-year-olds in mind and he has indicated (1969) that he devised the scheme to help his own young children to read. In addition, the approach was used in experimental conditions with infants, with older retarded pupils and also with educationally sub-normal children, apparently successfully. Accordingly, it appears to be intended for use with a fairly wide range of children of primary school age, although one would imagine that the interest level is more that of infants and young juniors than of older juniors.

D. OUTLINE OF THE APPROACH

I.   THE MEDIUM ITSELF

In *Colour Story Reading* the traditional spelling of English words is retained as well as capital letters and punctuation marks, in contrast to *Words in Colour* in which capital letters and most punctuation marks are dispensed with for the greater part of the course.

Two sample pages of the colour code used in *Colour Story Reading* are reproduced between pages 152–3. Only four colours are used for this code. The majority of the letters are printed in red, blue or green, while a few are in black against the normal background of white paper. In addition, certain of the single letters or groups of letters are printed in black on backgrounds of distinctive shape and colour; the colours red, blue and green each being used in the form of a square, a circle and a triangle, to create nine different background frames for the black letters. Thirteen ways of printing letters are thus available to represent the forty-two sounds which Jones identifies in the English language.

This obviously represents an entirely different kind of colour code from that of *Words in Colour*, in which forty-seven colours are used to represent forty-seven sounds, on the simple principle that one colour always represents the same sound. While Gattegno's code can rely on one rule, Jones' colour code necessarily requires more rules, if forty-two sounds are to be symbolized by a combination of twenty-six letters and thirteen ways of presenting them in print. The result is a code of fifty-three colour symbols, excluding black letters which need to be considered separately.

The code can only be fully understood by a careful study of the teacher's manual, supplemented by inspection of the children's books. Some idea of the form that the colour code takes, however, may be gained by outlining certain of its features and rules. The fifty-three colour symbols are as follows:

a.   fourteen single letters (a, e, i, y, o, u, m, p, r, s, c, j, g, and x) and one digraph (th) are printed in red;

b. fourteen single letters (i, y, o, u, t, h, v, w, b, z, s, k, c and g) and one digraph (qu) are printed in blue;

c. seven single letters (a, e, y, n, l, d and f) and seven digraphs (ch, gh, ph, oy, oi, ow and ou) are printed in green;

d. eight of the symbols on coloured background shapes represent eight sounds which can be spelt in a variety of ways; for example the red circle represents the 'er' sound, whether it is spelt 'er', 'ir', 'ur', 'ear' and so on;

e. the ninth coloured background, a blue circle, always represents a silent letter.

It can be noted that the forty-four symbols listed under (a), (b) and (c) require the child to pay attention to both the colour of a letter and its shape. If a child knows the relevant rules regarding, for instance, a letter 'c' printed in different colours, he can read the word 'cat' in which the 'c' is blue, the word 'nice' in which the 'c' is red, and the word 'which' in which the digraph 'ch' is green. On the other hand, as far as the nine symbols consisting of coloured backgrounds are concerned, the child only needs to know the rule regarding the colour and shape of the background and which sound it stands for. He need not pay any attention to the black letters printed on the coloured background. For example, if he knows that a red square represents the sound 'air', he need not note the actual letters forming the 'ae' at the beginning of 'aeroplane' or the 'are' at the end of 'square'. In this respect, the colour code of *Colour Story Reading* resembles that of *Words in Colour*.

A child's knowledge of the rules governing the fifty-three symbols already mentioned will indicate to him how he should pronounce the majority of regular words. Examples of the fifty-three relevant rules are that a red 's' stands for the sound 's' while a blue 's' stands for the sound 'z' and that any letters printed on a blue square say 'or'. The introduction of one additional symbol, however, breaks away from this rule of a symbol representing a clue to sound. Jones introduces a black letter on the normal background of the white page for what he terms 'non-conformist' letters. In the three children's books this black letter is used in the following words (the relevant letters have been printed in italics here):

Or*a*nge I*n*k *E*rnest o*f* s*a*id s*o*me the*y* w*a*s wh*a*t

An examination of this list inevitably raises a number of queries, but the first important point to notice is that the black letter serves a different function from the preceding fifty-three colour symbols. While the coloured symbols acted as clues to pronunciation, a black letter can only act as a danger signal and not as a clue. All it can do is indicate to the child that a letter is not pronounced as one might expect. It is this factor which makes it necessary to describe this particular colour code as a partial code rather than a complete code.

The device of the black letter is one which Jones has been driven to adopt owing to the limitations imposed by a partial code, which works reasonably well with many regular words but runs into difficulties with irregular words, including some of the commonest words in our language For instance, in the preceding list of nine irregular words, one notes that in 'was' and 'what', the letter 'a' sounds like 'o', a rule which applies to a number of other fairly common English words; but Jones has no means of indicating this. The same is true of 'f' sounding like 'v' and 'o' sounding like 'u'. In a complete code such as Gattegno's there is no problem: the 'f' would be coloured as a 'v', and so on; but a limited code such as Jones' is not capable of giving this sort of information.

The inclusion of the word 'they' in the list illustrates an additional difficulty in this code. The only way of depicting the long sound of 'a' is by using a red letter 'a'. This is employed in the word 'lazy' and again in the words 'made' and 'make', with the final 'e' in the latter two words being shown on blue circles to indicate that they are silent. Problems are encountered, however, when the same sound occurs in 'way', train' and 'they'. Nothing in the code focuses attention on the fact that the digraphs 'ay', 'ai' and 'ey', and other groups of letters such as 'eigh' are all different ways of spelling the sound of the long 'a'. When 'way' and 'train' are used in the text, the important digraphs are split; the 'a' in each case being printed in red and the 'y' and 'i' respectively being indicated as silent letters by printing them in black on blue circles. One suspects that such a procedure cannot help, and may even hinder, later acquisition of correct spelling rules.

Further problems arise when a digraph such as 'ow' can represent two different sounds, as in 'cow' and 'low'. This particular colour code fails to deal effectively with this situation. What it does is to print 'ow' green in 'cowboy' to correspond with 'ou' in 'loud', while in 'know' the 'w' is indicated as silent and the 'o' is printed in red to indicate the long 'o' sound. This represents an additional example of splitting important digraphs, in a manner unlikely to help the child to regard 'ow' as a specific group of letters with alternative pronunciations.

It is unnecessary to give further examples of the impossibility of presenting the forty-two or more sounds of English in a completely logical and regular manner, while retaining the traditional rules of English spelling with its many variations for one sound, by a colour code limited to only thirteen ways of printing the symbols. Such a code is only likely to function effectively with selected, regular words. It is bound to founder on many irregular words, and in the early reading materials certain words which would increase the problems are likely to be avoided. The same would be true of most other partial colour codes, although it does not follow that a partial code would not help the child who is beginning to learn to read. In fact, the code employed in *Colour Story Reading* does regularize many of the anomalies of ordinary t.o. and thus should greatly simplify the child's initial task.

The most important points to note regarding this colour code can be summarized as follows:

a.   it is a partial rather than a complete code;
b.   the colour code incorporates two different kinds of clues, one of which demands that both letter shape and colour should be considered, and the second of which only requires that attention should be paid to the shape and colour of the background while letter shape may be ignored;
c.   in many cases this colour code gives children clues to the pronunciation of words but in other cases it merely gives danger signals;
d.   in certain cases the code detracts attention from fairly common digraphs and phonic rules;
e.   as a decoding device, *Colour Story Reading* is not equipped to provide adequate clues to the pronunciation of many common irregular words.

2.   THE READING MATERIALS

a.   A teacher's book of stories

A book entitled *The Nineteen Stories*, meant to be read to the children by the teacher, forms the introduction to this approach. The stories concern Mr Nen and his five friends, Apple, Egg, Ink, Orange and Umbrella.

These stories use the vocabulary which will be employed in the children's reading books and introduce forty-two sounds associated with imagery. For instance, each of Mr Nen's five friends makes the sound of one of the short vowels when he speaks. In the second story, the consonants 't' and 'n' are introduced. The sound 'n' is made by a green net every time it catches a fish, a blue tin in which the fish is to be cooked makes the sound 't' as it becomes hot, and so on. By these means, children are provided, in story form, with visual images related to the sounds of letters – information which will later form a useful basis for learning the associations between written symbols and sounds. The nineteen stories are also recorded on three long-playing records.

b.   *Three children's reading books*

Three children's reading books, entitled *Mr Nen and His Friends*, Parts 1, 2 and 3, represent the only available* reading books for children printed in this colour code, although, since the author describes these as 'the first books to be published' in this code, one must assume that the intention is to publish additional books.

The subject matter of the stories is necessarily limited by both the nature of the vocabulary control and the small number of different words employed. The stories relate entirely to the subject matter of *The Nineteen Stories*, namely the activities of Mr Nen and his friends and the other letters and characters they meet.

The author does not suggest at precisely which stage the reading books should be given to the children but, as the first book refers to the first six stories to be read by the teacher, one imagines that the first reading book might be most profitably introduced after the children have heard these six stories.

The illustrations to be found on every page of the three books consist of pleasing, and sometimes amusing, line drawings in the four colours used in the text. The author points out that as these line drawings are essentially simple, children are able to copy them, and thereby the drawings open up a range of supplementary activities in which children can become involved.

The books are covered in linson cloth and the pages stapled together.

* Spring 1969.

The shape of the books is a horizontal rather than a vertical oblong, each book being about 9 inches by 6 inches (240 × 158 mm). This horizontal form is not usually as easy for infants to handle as a vertical form and, moreover, the books will take up a large area of space if two children sitting at one table want to open them out flat. On the other hand, the exceptional width of the page enables most of the sentences in the three books to be printed in a single line each, which is advantageous for beginning reading. In the third book, in which longer sentences extend over two lines of typescript, the phrasing is handled sensibly. The typescript is clear and the script 'a' and 'g' are used. The use of coloured letters makes the pages of print appear much more interesting than all black type, and one would imagine that children would find this use of colour attractive.

The first six pages in the first book consist entirely of illustrations captioned by their names: 'net', 'Des', 'Sam' and so on, together with the sounds they make, for example, Sam saying 's s s' and 'pot' saying 'p p p'. The sounds of letters continue to be used as captions for illustrations for some time. From page 7 onwards the text is in the form of complete sentences, such as 'This is a mat' and 'This is a lamp'. The repetitive nature of such sentences, together with the clear illustrations, provide children with helpful clues for reading the sentences. Moreover, in many cases certain of the words used in a sentence are adapted in the succeeding sentence to make a very easy gradient of difficulty, as shown in this group of sentences from the second book:

> Umbrella did jump.
> He made a big jump.
> He made a very big jump.

The vocabulary of the three children's reading books is as follows: Part 1 – twenty-six words, Part 2 – forty-five words, Part 3 – fifty words; making a total vocabulary load for the three books of 121 different words. Nearly all these words follow regular phonic rules, and a number of them, for example, 'Des', 'ram', 'huge', and 'phone' are not among the words which infants use most frequently in their own speech nor among the most common words found in children's or adult reading materials. Of course, as McNally and Murray (1962) have shown, many of our most commonly used words are irregular. *Colour Story Reading* uses thirty-eight of the 100 most common words in the English language, as listed by McNally and Murray, but certain very common words such as 'have', 'one', 'you', 'me', 'my', 'little', 'our', 'there', and 'want' are missing.

The small vocabulary load of the three children's books also leads to other weaknesses, although these may be found to have been overcome when additional books become available. For example, the common endings of words, 'ed', and 'ing', are entirely missing. Even more seriously certain symbols which are introduced are used in only one word, which would certainly not seem sufficient to ensure that children would remember them, unless a great deal of supplementary work were arranged by the teacher. For example, a blue triangle representing the very common sound 'sh' is employed throughout the entire scheme in only one word 'shop'. Similarly, 'ph', 'oy' and 'oi' are utilized in only one word each.

c.   A wall chart

One wall chart is available with *Colour Story Reading*. It takes the form of a reference chart of the coloured letters and symbols, and is intended to be used by the teacher and the children for reading and writing.

E.   SPECIAL FEATURES OF THE APPROACH

1.   One of the original features of *Colour Story Reading* is that children first encounter the sounds of letters in nineteen stories read to them by the teacher. The children are thus provided with interesting associations between the characters in the story and the sounds of letters, which enable them, at a later stage, to use imagery connected with the stories to reinforce and enliven the learning process of equating sounds with written symbols.

2.   The introduction of background shapes in different colours as identification symbols, in addition to letters printed in four colours, represents an innovation in colour codes.

3.   *Colour Story Reading* has been tried out with infants and older retarded readers and the reports of teachers are mainly favourable.

4. The reading attainments of children using *Colour Story Reading* are compared with the results of the use of ordinary t.o. and i.t.a. in two published research reports (Jones 1967a and 1968b). In both cases the results given are in favour of *Colour Story Reading*, although one is faced with a problem of interpreting these results satisfactorily; firstly, because many of the factors in the situations were not controlled, and, secondly, because *Colour Story Reading* was used for varying amounts of time, and in different ways, by different teachers.

F. ADDITIONAL FEATURES OF THE APPROACH

1. *Colour Story Reading* provides an easy gradient of introduction of sounds and words.

2. The small amount of reading materials available in this approach (namely three children's books), and the small total number of words introduced in the books mean that it covers less ground than any of the other eight approaches considered in Part 3 of this book. It may perhaps be regarded most appropriately as an introduction to beginning reading or as an aid to preliminary work in phonics.

3. The shortage of children's reading materials printed in this colour code might be compensated for, to some extent, by materials and activities provided by the teacher, along the lines of the suggestions put forward in the teacher's manual.

4. It is suggested that when children are writing they should be free to choose whether to write in one colour or in different colours.

G. OPTIMUM SITUATIONS

Until more reading materials become available in *Colour Story Reading*, it is difficult to consider its optimum use as a basic reading scheme. It will probably be found most suitable as an introduction to reading or as supplementary materials for children who have begun with a look-and-say reading approach, in the following circumstances:

1. with children in infant or lower junior classes and with younger children in educationally sub-normal schools;

2. with younger retarded pupils in remedial situations, as they would be likely to be attracted by the novelty of the stories and the intriguing appearance of books printed in colour;

3. by a teacher who believes that the inconsistencies of the English spelling system constitute one of the major stumbling blocks when children are learning to read;

4. by a teacher who believes in some form of phonic training but who prefers an approach which does not consist of formal drill.

SUGGESTIONS FOR FURTHER READING

(Referring to *Colour Story Reading*)

In the following article, Mr Jones, the author of *Colour Story Reading*, describes the results of an investigation into the value of colour as an aid to the visual discrimination of words and letters.

JONES, J. K. (1965) 'Colour as an aid to visual perception in early reading.' *British Journal of Educational Psychology*, Vol. 35, No. 1, pp. 22–27.

An account of his research project, sponsored by the Department of Education and Science, into the value of phonetic colour in early reading is given in:

JONES, J. K. (1967a) *Colour Story Reading: A Research Report*. London: Nelson.

Of the following two articles, the first provides a description of *Colour Story Reading*, while the second compares the reading results of Jones' own experiment with *Colour Story Reading* with the results of children using i.t.a. in Downing's second i.t.a. experiment.

JONES, J. K. (1968a) 'Phonetic colour reading.' In DOWNING, J. A. and BROWN, A. L. (eds.) *The Third International Reading Symposium*. London: Cassell.

JONES, J. K. (1968b) 'Comparing i.t.a. with Colour Story Reading.' *Educational Research*, Vol. 10, No. 3, pp. 226–234.

3. i.t.a. (The Initial Teaching Alphabet)
(Pitman, J., 1959)

A. i.t.a. IS A MEDIUM

Before examining *i.t.a.* within the framework used in the assessment of the preceding approaches to reading, one important point must be established. *i.t.a.* is not a method of teaching but solely a medium, in the form of a simplified and regularized spelling system, designed for beginning reading. It differs from every other approach considered in this book, in that it does not relate only to one particular reading scheme or set of reading apparatus, and is thus not tied to either a look-and-say or to a phonic method.

B. THE INVENTOR

I. BACKGROUND

Sir James Pitman, the designer of *i.t.a.*, is the grandson of the late Sir Isaac Pitman who invented Pitman's shorthand and also designed an augmented alphabet known as 'Phonotypy'. Sir James Pitman was for many years a Member of Parliament and chairman and managing director of the publishing firm of Sir Isaac Pitman & Sons Ltd. He has always been particularly interested in phonetics, linguistics and alphabet reform. Although he has served on the committee of the Simplified Spelling Society, his invention of *i.t.a.* was not intended as a proposal for the reform of English spelling but primarily as a medium for beginning reading. Sir James Pitman was a member of the committee which was set up in 1960 under the auspices of the National Foundation for Educational Research and the Institute of Education of London University, to initiate and guide the research project to investigate the effectiveness of *i.t.a.* as a means of beginning reading in schools.

2.   BASIC BELIEFS

In the other approaches examined, the authors have revealed their own
beliefs about reading by the kind of materials they have produced, and by
their suggestions regarding ways in which the materials might be utilized.
From this evidence it has been possible to deduce whether the authors'
basic beliefs about reading tuition favoured incidental learning or systematic teaching. When considering *i.t.a.*, however, the question of basic
beliefs couched in these terms is not relevant. What does emerge quite
clearly from Pitman's own writings is his belief that the irregularities of
traditional orthography constitute a major stumbling block to children's
reading progress. Teachers who adopt *i.t.a.* need to share this view but
they may differ in their leanings towards either systematic or incidental
tuition.

3.   TEACHER'S MANUALS

Because *i.t.a.* is not an approach represented by a single set of reading
materials, as is the case with *Words in Colour* or *Colour Story Reading*, no
one particular teacher's manual can be examined in this context, as has
been done with other approaches. Some of the reading schemes devised
specifically for *i.t.a.*, however, are accompanied by teacher's manuals or
notes: for example, three infant schemes, *The Downing Reading Scheme*
(Downing 1963), *Early to Read Series* (Mazurkiewicz and Tanyzer 1963)
and *Oldham Readers* (Harrison 1966), and one remedial reading scheme,
Clearway Readers (Bell 1965).

In addition, there are numerous publications describing the alphabet
and its use, as well as innumerable research reports giving details and results
of wide-scale experiments in schools. A selection of these publications is
given in 'Suggestions for Further Reading' at the end of Part 3 of this
chapter, together with details of the i.t.a. Foundation which has been set
up to advise and train teachers who are interested in *i.t.a.* and those who
wish to use it. As well as giving general advice and answering queries, the
Foundation arranges courses and workshops on *i.t.a.* for teachers in various
parts of the country, and runs correspondence courses for teachers who are
unable to attend the workshops. There is thus no lack of information on
i.t.a. available for teachers.

C. THE SCOPE OF THE APPROACH

I. A TOTAL APPROACH

i.t.a. represents a total approach to beginning reading, as the learner needs to rely solely on *i.t.a.* script – as far as both reading and writing are concerned – until such time as he is ready to transfer to t.o. This means that in the early stages neither published books nor handwritten materials in t.o. are expected to be employed.

2. THE RANGE OF READING ATTAINMENTS

i.t.a. is only meant to be employed in the initial stages of learning to read and write. At a certain stage, when fluency in reading *i.t.a.* is achieved, the learner transfers to books printed in t.o. This stage is normally reached within the range of one to three years, although with a small minority of children this period can be less than one year or more than three years. In 1967 Downing quoted 152 pupils who had learnt to read using *i.t.a.* and who had been transferred to t.o. books by their teachers at least six weeks prior to the administration of these t.o. tests, as having average scores when tested on the Neale (1958) *Analysis of Reading Ability*. These correspond to reading ages of eight years five months for accuracy and seven years eight months for comprehension. Accordingly, *i.t.a.* can be considered as a medium for use from the very earliest stages of beginning reading up to a reading age of about eight.

3. INTENDED PUPILS

i.t.a. was first used with infants, including children only four years of age. At the same time it was expected to prove useful for failing readers in junior classes and secondary modern schools. It has been used with pupils of all levels of ability, including children in educationally sub-normal special schools, as well as with retarded readers in remedial groups and with adult illiterates.

In all the preceding groups, English was the spoken language of those learning to read by means of *i.t.a.* A special form of *i.t.a.* has also been devised for use with people whose native language is not English.

Thus *i.t.a.* was intended to have a wide range of applicability, for all pupils who are beginning readers, regardless of their ages or situations.

D. OUTLINE OF THE APPROACH

I.   THE RATIONALE UNDERLYING THIS ALPHABET

Both Pitman and Downing have expounded at length on the rationale underlying this particular augmented alphabet. While recognizing that any attempt to describe the main points simply will probably fail to do full justice to the ideas of the inventor, it is nevertheless hoped that the following summary may be found useful by teachers and students who are not acquainted with *i.t.a.* The basis of reasoning which led to the invention of *i.t.a.* appears to run somewhat as follows.

a.   The irregularities of the traditional English spelling system constitute a major cause of difficulty for the beginning reader.

b.   The form of alphabet which would do most to facilitate beginning reading would have one written symbol, and only one, to represent each of the spoken sounds of English. With such an alphabet, one single rule of spelling could exist, based on a one-to-one correspondence between grapheme and phoneme.

c.   To devise such an alphabet would not be too difficult, especially if one had a free hand to make a fresh start. The Shaw Alphabet, for instance, represents one example of such an alphabet, although it is intended as a complete reform of the English spelling system rather than a medium for beginning reading.

d.   In devising a simplified spelling system intended only for beginning reading, it would be unwise to produce one which diverged too far from the traditional alphabet and spelling system, as children who had to transfer from one system to the other would be likely to experience difficulties.

e.   As the traditional alphabet has only twenty-six letters to represent some forty sounds found in the spoken English language, any new alphabet which attempts a close correspondence between grapheme and phoneme must necessarily introduce new written characters.

f.   In devising a new code, the adoption of the following three rules will help to facilitate the transfer from the new medium to t.o. First, as many of the traditional letters of the alphabet as possible should be retained. Secondly, in designing additional characters, reference should be made to the appearance of traditionally spelt words so that the new words will resemble them as closely as possible. In this respect, the outline of the upper half of words is particularly important because when fluent readers are 'skimming' print they rely heavily on the top 'coastline' of words. Thirdly, changes in spelling rules, if such are to be introduced, should be linked with the rules of the traditional spelling system.

g. The requirement of ease of transition may necessitate certain deviations from the desired principle of a one-to-one correspondence between written symbol and spoken sound.

Reasoning along the foregoing lines led Pitman to the invention of his Augmented Roman Alphabet (A.R.), which was later renamed the Initial Teaching Alphabet (i.t.a.). It was developed to a certain extent from his grandfather's 'Phonotopy', with many modifications and amendments demanded by the rationale underlying it. In contrast to the accounts of the development of the colour codes employed in *Words in Colour* and *Colour Story Reading*, it is interesting to note that with this particular medium no pilot studies were undertaken with young children in order to ascertain whether modifications to the proposed alphabet might be necessary. In the event, during the first year or so of using A.R. in schools, only one or two minor amendments to it were made. Certain suggestions, however, have been put forward, for example by Stott (1964) and Downing (1967a and b) that additional modifications might still be desirable.

2.   DESCRIPTION OF THE MEDIUM

a.   A simplified spelling system

In the terms used in this book, *i.t.a.* is classified as a 'simplified spelling system', although Mountford (1964 and 1965) and Downing (1967a) prefer to describe it as a 'writing system'. Although it does not establish a one-to-one correspondence between written symbol and spoken sound as was originally claimed, for example by Downing (1962), it does go a long way towards this principle, by eliminating many of the irregularities found in t.o. It would be quite fair to claim that the *general* rule is a one-to-one correspondence between written symbol and spoken sound, though there are exceptions. Moreover, as Pitman (1959) points out, *i.t.a.* leaves 50 per cent of t.o. words 'virtually unchanged' while a further 10 per cent have only minor modifications such as the omission of an 'e' from the word 'have'.

b.   Two minor features of the alphabet

In the early publications of both Pitman and Downing, much was made of the difficulties faced by children when capital letters which differ from their lower case appearance are used, and also when two forms of lower case 'a' and 'g' are employed in different reading materials. On these grounds, *i.t.a.* discards the normal form of upper case letters and utilizes in their place a slightly larger form of the lower case letters. In addition, only the script form of 'g' is used, while the two types of 'a' are used to represent the two different sounds found in 'cat' and 'father', which are printed in *i.t.a.* as cat and father.

Teachers may consider these to be the two least important aspects of *i.t.a.* The adoption of the script 'a' and 'g' for instance, is now fairly common practice in reading materials published in t.o. for beginning readers. Regarding the difficulties occasioned by the employment of those upper case letters which differ from the corresponding lower case letters, teachers and educators are not in agreement on the importance of this factor. For example, Miss Wignall, an infant head teacher, writing in Stott (1964) says, 'We have never found that capital letters need much formal teaching to average children who are used to seeing them in their reading books, on large classroom newsheets, on their name-cards and all around them as they walk past shops, bus stops, advertisements and, of course, when watching television.' If this factor were considered important by the majority of teachers, it would be a comparatively simple matter to adopt lower case letters in the publication of t.o. reading materials for the early stages of learning and to introduce them later in the reading programme as, for instance, Gattegno does in *Words in Colour*.

c.   The alphabet itself

The original Augmented Roman Alphabet consisted of forty-three characters, but later one further character was added. A list of the forty-four characters of *i.t.a.* is shown on page 181, and a passage of prose

The Alphabet of i.t.a.[1]

a	ɑ	æ	au	b	c	ch
apple	father	angel	author	bed	cat	chair

d	ɛɛ	e	f	g	h	ie
doll	eel	egg	finger	girl	hat	tie

i	j	k	l	m	n	ŋ
ink	jam	kitten	lion	man	nest	king

œ	o	ω	ꞷ	ou	ɔi	p
toe	on	book	food	out	oil	pig

r	ɾ	s	ʃh	3	t	th
red	bird	soap	ship	treasure	tree	three

th	ue	u	v	w	wh	y
mother	due	up	van	window	wheel	yellow

z	ʒ
zoo	is

printed in *i.t.a.* on page 182. Twenty-four of the characters are letters from the traditional alphabet, letters 'x' and 'q' having been omitted. The letter 'd' has been altered slightly by the extension of the vertical stroke downwards to help children to distinguish it from the letter 'b'. This represents one of the amendments made to the original alphabet as a result of practical experience with young children. Of the twenty additional characters, one is the alternative form of letter 'a' mentioned earlier and fifteen represent amalgamations of letters forming digraphs, for example, 'ie', 'au', 'sh', and 'th'. The most radical change from t.o., and probably the one which will prove of most help to the learner, is the availability of seventeen vowel characters in *i.t.a.* Details of how the characters should be written are given in Downing (1964).

[1] From *An Introduction to the Initial Teaching Alphabet*, i.t.a. Foundation Publication No. 1.

A Sample of Prose in i.t.a.[1]

ſhe nekst þiŋ tω dω woſ
tω fiend a plæs for ſhe scωl,
and ernest ωul choeſ a littl ſhed
nekst tω ſhe stæbl whær emily ſhe
gœt livd. "ſhat will bee very
uesfωl," hee tœld himself,
"becauſ emily can provied milk
for ſhe littl wunſ in ſhe
morniŋ." and when hee askt
emily, ſhee sed ſhee wωd bee
very pleeſd tω dω it.

The spelling rules employed with *i.t.a.* are slightly more complicated than might be realized at first glance. The teacher considering the adoption of *i.t.a.* should refer to Mountford (1964 and 1965) on this point. It is preferable to consider the deviations from the principle of regularity of grapheme–phoneme correspondence separately, according to how they are likely to affect children's reading and writing.

d.   *i.t.a. as a decoding device*

i.t.a. was designed as a decoding device, that is, as an alphabet which would simplify the process of learning to read. Accordingly, it should be considered first in this respect.

As far as decoding is concerned, the general rule applicable to *i.t.a.* is that each written symbol represents one sound. Deviations from this

[1] From *Blackberry Farm Stories* by Jane Pilgrim – Book 1: *Ernest Owl Starts a School;* published by University of London Press Ltd.

general rule are mainly of a minor nature. For example, double letters are retained in words such as 'little' or 'running'. Secondly, the letter 'y' can be pronounced either as in 'yes' or 'silly'. Most infant teachers would agree that both these points occasion children little difficulty in reading either t.o. or *i.t.a.*

Two further deviations from the general rule of a one-to-one correspondence between grapheme and phoneme are probably more important, and both are the result of the attempt to refrain from making radical alterations to the traditional spelling of words. The first is that no special character is used to represent the indeterminate vowel sound found in 'the', '*a*', 'ribbon', 'or*a*nge', 'open', and so on. A number of linguists and educationists, for example Stott (1964), have criticized *i.t.a.* on this score. It should also be noted that in this respect both *Colour Story Reading* and *i.t.a.* differ from *Words in Colour*, in which this sound is always represented by one particular colour. The second feature which may cause children a certain amount of initial difficulty in decoding *i.t.a.* relates to those awkward English words involving the 'er' sound. The character '*r*' for example, appears only in combination with certain other vowel characters in words such as 'he*r*', 'bi*r*d', and 'absu*r*d', in which the vowel preceding '*r*' is not pronounced. On the other hand, neither of these deviations from the general rule of one grapheme representing one sound can have very serious implications for decoding, as most teachers' reports on *i.t.a.* indicate that once a child has mastered the primary sounds of the forty-four characters he experiences little difficulty in decoding any of the words he attempts to read.

e.   i.t.a. as an encoding device

The other two media examined in this chapter, *Words in Colour* and *Colour Story Reading*, have been considered solely as decoding devices. This was because, in each case, the use of a colour code for reading does not alter the fact that children's free writing is in t.o., although in the case of *Colour Story Reading* children can employ the code by writing with coloured pencils if they wish. In contrast, *i.t.a.* is employed as an encoding as well as a decoding device; children write in this new alphabet and not in t.o.

Examined pedantically, the spelling rules of *i.t.a.* demonstrate more alternative choices likely to affect writing than reading. Most of the deviations mentioned in relation to decoding are also likely to affect encoding. In addition, the following are some of the alternatives with which, in theory, a child will be faced when he wishes to write words in *i.t.a.* The 'k' sound may be represented as 'c', 'k' or 'ck'; the sound 'j' can be written in five different ways in 'jelly', 'adjust', 'bridge', 'soldier' and 'procedure'; the sound 'ch' is written in four different ways in 'much', 'match', 'question' and 'nature'; the 'er' sound is written differently in 'bird', 'herd' and 'word'; and the 'or' sound is written in three different ways.

In practice, it does not work out like this, for two reasons. First, the young child who begins to write soon after he begins to read rarely realizes that there are alternative spellings of certain sounds available to him. He selects from the forty-four characters which he has learnt to associate with forty-four sounds the one which represents the sound he wants to write. Moreover, Pitman and Downing have always advised teachers to accept from children, in their early free writing, any of the alternative graphemes for a phoneme. Thus the child who writes 'kat' instead of 'cat' would have this accepted. Furthermore, even at a later stage when a child is aware of alternative spellings for certain sounds, the choices are few compared with the large range in t.o. It is interesting to note that although *i.t.a.* was planned with the aim of simplifying the decoding process, its beneficial effects on encoding have been reported by teachers and researchers as frequently as have its effects on decoding. For example, Warburton and Southgate (1969) report that many teachers who had used *i.t.a.* rated its beneficial effect on children's free writing as its main advantage.

E. METHODS

When *i.t.a.* was first used in schools, both Pitman and Downing emphasized that with this medium a teacher could use any method she preferred. Downing (1962), for instance, posed the question, 'Does the teacher have to modify her methods of teaching reading if she uses A.R.?' His reply to his own question was: ' "No" is the brief answer to this question, although some adaptations may be forced upon the teacher by the nature of A.R. However, in general it is true to say that teaching methods can remain as usual.'

In fact, when the first experiment commenced in England in 1961, the only reading scheme then available in *i.t.a.* was a transliterated version of the *Janet and John* (O'Donnell and Munro 1961) scheme. As this is a look-and-say scheme, teachers had little choice but to begin reading tuition with a look-and-say method. Warburton and Southgate (1969), reporting on the use of *i.t.a.* between 1961 and 1966, note that from among all the *i.t.a.* classes visited only one teacher used a phonic method as the initial method. (In the U.S.A., in contrast, most teachers using *i.t.a.* begin with phonics.) All the other teachers interviewed began with a look-and-say method, and all introduced some phonic training either systematically or incidentally at varying stages in the reading programme. Moreover, many teachers reported that the regularities of the alphabet itself appeared to make children more interested in the relationships between sounds and symbols, and in phonic rules, than was common when t.o. had been used. These teachers had found themselves involved in phonic work at an earlier stage than usual, not because of their own decisions to do so, but as a result of the children's interest and initiative.

More recently, a report by Tudor-Hart (1969) of an experiment in which different groups of children were taught to read in *i.t.a.* by different methods concludes that *i.t.a.* is more effective when a phonic rather than a look-and-say method is used.

F.   CHILDREN'S READING MATERIALS

The use of *i.t.a.*, in contrast to the two colour codes examined earlier, does not restrict the teacher's choice of reading materials for her pupils to one limited set of materials or one reading scheme. Since 1961, when the first books printed in *i.t.a.* were published in Great Britain, steadily increasing quantities of children's books and reading apparatus in *i.t.a.* have been published every year. The book list issued by the i.t.a. Foundation in December 1968 (*The i.t.a. Journal* No. 14) lists some 750 titles of children's reading books published in *i.t.a.* These include basic reading schemes, book corner books of varying levels of difficulty, reference books and so on. In addition, there are 'Number Books for Beginning Mathematics' and numerous work books and reading apparatus of different kinds. Many of the beginning reading books originally published in *i.t.a.* were transliterations of existing t.o. books, but a growing number of publications are now being written especially for *i.t.a.*

The i.t.a. Foundation's book list gives details of nine 'Beginning Reading Schemes'. These vary in size from one comprising seven small children's books to others which include basic books, supplementary stories, work books and all kinds of supporting materials in the form of pictures, cards, and so on. In addition there are five schemes described as 'Remedial Reading Schemes'. Of this total of fourteen reading schemes, nine are transliterations of t.o. schemes, and they include both look-and-say and phonic approaches. The remaining five schemes were devised specifically for *i.t.a.*, and they also include both look-and-say and phonic approaches.

One further point which should be noted about reading materials printed in *i.t.a.* is that they are usually slightly more expensive than when the same books are printed in t.o.

G. SPECIAL FEATURES OF *i.t.a.*

1. *i.t.a.* is the only medium other than t.o. for teaching the early stages of reading in English in which a large selection of published reading materials are available.

2. This wide range of reading materials means that teachers choosing to use *i.t.a.* can hold different basic beliefs, adopt different roles, support different methods and favour different procedures.

3. Large numbers of children have been involved in experiments using *i.t.a.* and the results have usually been favourable. The main conclusions drawn are that the use of *i.t.a.* makes learning to read easier and speedier in the initial stages than does the use of t.o., but that by the age of eight the reading standards of children taught by t.o. are similar to those of children taught by *i.t.a.*

4. In addition to these experiments, *i.t.a.* has been used extensively in normal conditions in schools, and the teachers concerned have generally reported favourably on it in comparison with t.o. (Sceats 1967, and

Warburton and Southgate 1969). Teacher's comments have also emphasized the pleasure and satisfaction which the earlier and easier reading has given the children themselves.

5. As *i.t.a.* is a simplified encoding device as well as a decoding device, its use enables the child to express his own ideas in writing more easily than if he were using t.o. or colour codes in which there are many more alternative graphemes available for each phoneme.

6. The use of *i.t.a.*, in contrast to the two colour codes examined, brings with it the problem of children having to make the transfer to traditional spelling in both reading and writing. Reports on this transfer, as far as reading is concerned, differ. Downing (1967a and 1967b) notes a set-back at the stage of transition in reading, but most teachers report that children experience no practical difficulty in this respect. It is generally concluded that the transition in spelling should take place later than the transition in reading, and that it is helpful if children are given definite tuition regarding t.o. spelling rules. The question of transition from *i.t.a.* to t.o. may cause problems if a child who has started to learn to read with *i.t.a.* is moved to a t.o. school before he is ready to transfer from *i.t.a.*

H. OPTIMUM SITUATIONS

With the other eight approaches to reading considered in this chapter, it has been possible to suggest situations in which they might be used to the best advantage. This was made possible by the fact that in each case there were limiting factors such as the author's basic belief, the method employed the age of intended pupils and so on. As *i.t.a.* is not tied to any one method or one set of reading materials, optimum situations cannot be suggested as in the case of the other approaches. All that can be noted is that it has a wider range of applicability than many of the other approaches and can be used effectively by teachers holding different beliefs, with pupils of different ages and abilities, in a variety of situations.

Only one suggestion can be tentatively put forward. It may be that as *i.t.a.* represents a total approach to reading and utilizes a medium other than t.o., it could prove more effective with infants and with entire classes of retarded or backward pupils, or of adult illiterates, than with those remedial groups of junior and secondary children who spend most of their time in their normal classes, where they will be surrounded by t.o. On the other hand, there is an advantage in using something entirely new for remedial reading with failing readers, and there are reports of *i.t.a.* being used successfully with such groups.

SUGGESTIONS FOR FURTHER READING

(Referring to *i.t.a.*)

There have been so many publications referring to *i.t.a.* that the selection of a small sample for further reading is far from easy. The following list consists of some of the simpler accounts of the medium itself, practical suggestions for using this medium, the conclusions of teachers who have used it, and a few research reports.

The first four publications in the following list, if read in the order given, should provide a useful introduction to *i.t.a.* for the teacher or student who is not acquainted with this medium. The fifth one is a reference list which most teachers using *i.t.a.* will want to keep by them. The final two pamphlets offer help to the teacher regarding spelling in *i.t.a.*

An Introduction to the Initial Teaching Alphabet. London: i.t.a. Foundation.

DOWNING, J. A. (1964) *The Initial Teaching Alphabet: Explained and Illustrated.* London: Cassell.

LEIGH, T. (1967) *i.t.a. in the Classroom.* Edinburgh: Chambers.

HARRISON, M. (1964) *Instant Reading: The Story of the Initial Teaching Alphabet.* London: Pitman.

i.t.a. Word List. London: i.t.a. Foundation.

MOUNTFORD, J. (1964) *Short Notes for Reference on i.t.a. Transliteration.* Edinburgh: Chambers.

MOUNTFORD, J. (1965) *i.t.a. as a Grading Device.* Edinburgh: Chambers.

Reports of the first British experiment with *i.t.a.* are given in the following two publications, the first of which includes evaluations of this experiment by eleven well-known contributors:

DOWNING, J. A. (1967a) *The i.t.a. Symposium*. Slough: National Foundation for Educational Research.

DOWNING, J. A. (1967b) *Evaluating the Initial Teaching Alphabet*. London: Cassell.

The following report records the result of an experiment in which *i.t.a.* was used with remedial reading groups:

GEORGIADES, N. J. (1969) *The Initial Teaching Alphabet in Remedial Reading Groups*. London: Harrap.

The ways in which teachers actually used *i.t.a.* in schools and their comments on its value, as well as the difficulties they encountered and how they overcame them, are described in:

SCEATS, J. (1967) *i.t.a. and the Teaching of Literacy*. London: The Bodley Head.

In the following report, sponsored by the Schools Council, the authors evaluate evidence collected from some 400 teachers, advisers, inspectors, lecturers, parents and others who had either used *i.t.a.* or observed it in use, and make a critical appraisal of seventeen pieces of research on *i.t.a.*

WARBURTON, F. W. and SOUTHGATE, V. (1969). *i.t.a.: An Independent Evaluation*. Edinburgh: Chambers, and London: Murray.

A complete list of all British and many American publications on *i.t.a.*, as well as details of children's reading materials in *i.t.a.*, can be obtained from the Initial Teaching Alphabet Foundation, 154 Southampton Row, London W.C.1.

4. A Brief Comparison of the Three Media

The teacher who, after reading chapter 5, decided that the possibility of using a new medium was worth exploring, might find it helpful if the main differences between the three media just examined are now summarized.

The most obvious point of divergence is that *Words in Colour* and *Colour Story Reading* represent examples of signalling systems, both employing colour codes, while *i.t.a.* constitutes a simplified spelling system. The two colour codes also contrast with each other as *Words in Colour* is a complete code while *Colour Story Reading* is a partial code. Some teachers may be hesitant about the use of a colour code because of doubts concerning its practicability for children who suffer from colour blindness. Evidence on this point is scarce but reports from teachers who have used either *Words in Colour* or *Colour Story Reading* do not refer to children encountering difficulties on this score. Jones (1967) in his teacher's manual for *Colour Story Reading* notes that about 8 per cent of males suffer from some form of defective colour vision, although this does not mean that they are unable to distinguish between colours but merely that they see them differently from people with normal vision. He states that, 'Complete colour blindness, monochromism, occurs in about one person in a million.' Moreover, it should be noted that with both *Words in Colour* and *Colour Story Reading* ordinary black print is used alongside the colour code; with *Words in Colour* only the wall charts are in the colour code.

When methods are considered, it will be found that *Words in Colour* and *Colour Story Reading* both use phonic methods, but that the former lays down explicit directions for both method and teaching techniques, while the latter is more flexible. In contrast, *i.t.a.* is not tied to method but can be used with either a phonic or a look-and-say method. When reading materials are considered, the threeapproaches group themselves differently. *Words in Colour* and *i.t.a.* should be regarded as total approaches, as children's early reading experiences are expected to be limited to reading materials printed in the respective media. In contrast, it appears possible to use *Colour Story Reading* alongside other reading materials printed in t.o.

In chapter 5 it was suggested that beginning reading tuition in t.o., whether it commenced with a look-and-say or a phonic method, presented the child with the same difficulty, as in both cases he was bound to meet two kinds of words, regular and irregular, which needed to be tackled in different ways. It was further suggested that new media were developed in order to prevent the child from being faced with this problem. Accordingly, of each new medium, one should first consider the extent to which it succeeds in providing the child with a uniform method of decoding unknown words. Secondly, one should probe for any evidence of complications or disadvantages, and equally of possible additional bonuses, which necessarily accompany the solution to this problem. (The reader might find it helpful at this point to refer to the summary of the advantages and disadvantages of regularized media which are listed in chapter 5, pages 48 and 49.)

Words in Colour employs a complete and absolutely consistent colour code, so that any child who masters it develops a uniform method of reading unknown words printed in this code. The exercises which form an integral part of the approach will help the child to recognize letters in black print and reinforce his knowledge of the sounds they represent; they will also give him flexibility in analysing and recombining both phonemes and graphemes in a manner that will lead to an appreciation of t.o. spelling rules. To achieve this effect, the teacher's own flexibility of approach must be largely sacrificed. She must be willing to follow the rules laid down for her guidance, to confine children's reading materials to a limited set of books and apparatus, and to divorce reading tuition in the early stages from the other activities of the class.

Colour Story Reading, although it does not provide either a complete code or an absolutely consistent method of attempting to decode unknown words, does supply a partial colour code which will help the child by overcoming some of the anomalies of ordinary t.o. and by drawing attention to certain of the phonic regularities and conventions of t.o. In contrast to *Words in Colour*, it represents only a brief introductory course to beginning reading; it allows the teacher freedom to utilize it either as supplementary or basic materials and to choose other reading materials for use alongside it and it presents the child with colourful books.

Neither does *i.t.a.* provide an absolutely complete and regular code for decoding new words, as does *Words in Colour*, but it approaches much more closely to this level than does *Colour Story Reading*. It has the advantage over *Words in Colour* in that teachers can choose to use any method and any procedures they prefer, and select what they consider to be the most appropriate reading schemes and supporting materials. Moreover, children's reading and writing can arise from, and be integrated with, all that is going on in the class, the school and beyond. *i.t.a.* also has one other important advantage over both *Words in Colour* and *Colour Story Reading*, as it presents a fairly regular encoding system which teachers have found to be a definite incentive to children's free writing.

On the other hand, with *i.t.a.* there are two drawbacks which certain teachers may consider important and which do not apply to the two colour codes. First, with *i.t.a.* the alphabet used in school is different from the one used outside. Secondly, children have eventually to transfer from *i.t.a.* to t.o. both in reading and spelling, a problem which does not exist with the colour codes, as children use black print in t.o. alongside the colour code. While in normal circumstances the stage of transfer from *i.t.a.* to t.o. does not appear to cause children difficulty, it may do so if the transition is hastened by an unwise teacher or if the child has to be transferred suddenly to a school which uses only t.o.

The three appraisals of reading approaches employing new media have shown that each of them has certain advantages over the use of ordinary t.o., although the advantages of the three respective media are not by any means identical. Moreover, in every case there exist certain drawbacks to set against the advantages. Whether to use a new medium, and if so which one to choose, can only be judged by the individual head teacher, against her background of basic beliefs and preferred method and procedures.

PART FOUR
Conclusions

11 The teacher's choice

The purpose of this book has been to help teachers to make a rational choice from among the many new approaches to beginning reading which are available. One of the authors' objectives has been to show that the choice of an approach to reading necessitates much more than merely glancing through new reading schemes and selecting on such superficial evidence as the attractiveness of the pictures or the size of the print. Certainly a close examination of books and apparatus is advisable, but this should be undertaken only as the final step in a process of selection, which has involved making a number of important decisions.

Some teachers may be disappointed that a chapter has not been devoted to results of experiments comparing different approaches to reading, which might either wholly or partially have enabled them to make a choice. Although certain research findings are mentioned, both in the text and in the lists of suggestions for further reading, this aspect has not been further extended because few adequate studies have been undertaken which compare the results obtained when different approaches to beginning reading are used. The use of the word 'adequate' here is related to the multiplicity of factors influencing reading progress which have been emphasized throughout this book. By 'adequate studies' are meant those in which sufficient of the most important variables are controlled as to make it feasible to attribute the different results obtained to the use of the approaches in question. One example will suffice to illustrate this point. Suppose there are two matched groups of children, and that Teacher A is using Approach 1 and Teacher B is using Approach 2. Suppose also that Teacher A believes in an early start to reading and Teacher B believes in a delayed beginning. If, after a specified period the reading standards in Class A are much better than in Class B, does this lead us to conclude that

Approach 1 is 'better' than Approach 2? Could the different results not be just as easily attributed to the teachers' different beliefs, resulting in different emphases on reading and the time devoted to it, or to the teachers' different abilities or to any of the other factors in the situation which were not matched or controlled in any way?

Setting up experiments to compare the results of using different approaches to beginning reading, especially in British primary schools with their wide range of procedures, is a much more complicated business than is often appreciated. Furthermore, most teachers cannot be expected to be experts in evaluating experimental designs and, consequently, the results emanating from the experiments. Until such time as more sophisticated experiments are undertaken to compare the results of using different approaches, and until research workers have become more skilled at writing about these results in straightforward, non-technical language, (as well as at developing the practical implications for teachers and children), research findings are unlikely to provide much help for the teacher who is posing the question of 'Reading – which approach?'.

As neither of the extreme plans of selection, namely superficial examination of reading materials nor selection based exclusively on research results, constitutes a useful course of action, the authors have proposed a middle-of-the-road plan of selection. It involves a developmental procedure based on certain criteria, applied in a specified order, which will progressively narrow the field of choice until an appropriate solution becomes clear. It is hoped that teachers will consider the suggested selection plan to be sensible and practical.

Part 2 of this book, 'Criteria For Assessing Reading Approaches', places before the reader many of the factors which influence children's reading progress and thus have a bearing upon the selection of an approach to beginning reading. Obviously some of these factors exert greater influence than others. However, the two most important are considered to be the teacher's own basic beliefs about reading and the needs of the children at each stage of learning to read. When these two factors have been examined and the relevant decisions taken, the choice of medium and method will be simplified, and an examination of the relevant materials will become more purposeful. The detailed plan of appraisal of reading approaches outlined in Part 2 of the book should prove equally as useful for application to forthcoming approaches as to those currently available.

Some readers may be daunted by the complexity of the choice and some may think that it would be impossible to consider every point that has been listed. Nevertheless, each one of these points forms part of the whole critical appraisal of an approach, and it would not be untrue to say that many experienced teachers do consider, in some cases almost unconsciously, a vast range of details relating to the uses to which they will put the selected approach. The young or inexperienced teacher will eventually build up a facility for examining reading materials with incisive insight, and the suggestions put forward in this book will help her to organize and clarify her latent ideas on the teaching of reading.

In Part 3 of the book, in order to exemplify the techniques of appraisal suggested in Part 2, nine current approaches to reading are examined in detail. The selection of these particular approaches does not imply that they are the most noteworthy approaches to beginning reading at present available. They have been selected, three in each of the main divisions of look-and-say, phonic, and use of media other than t.o., because they form interesting contrasts to each other, and because the differences between them serve to illustrate many of the points made in Part 2. The teacher who has considered these nine appraisals will find it rewarding to apply the same techniques to other approaches in which she is interested.

Throughout this book the authors have expressed their conviction that no one approach to reading can be considered as the ideal choice in every situation. They have tried to show that most approaches have certain advantages and that all have some disadvantages. It is only the head teacher and the class teacher who can make the final choice regarding medium, method and reading materials. The teacher who has considered the criteria of selection and made the necessary decisions in the order suggested should succeed in selecting one or more approaches which are particularly appropriate to her own beliefs and the needs of the children concerned. If it should happen that all who read this book arrive at the same answer to the question, 'Reading – which approach?', the authors will realize, with disappointment, that they have failed in the task which they set themselves!

BIBLIOGRAPHY AND APPENDIX

Bibliography

ASHLEY, E. (1938) *The Mac and Tosh Readers*. Huddersfield: Schofield & Sims, Ltd.

BELL, S. E. (1965) *Clearway Readers*. London: Initial Teaching Publishing Co.

BERG, L. *et al*. (1969) *Nippers*. London: Macmillan.

BLEASDALE, E. and W. (1967) *Reading by Rainbow*. Bolton: Moor Platt Press.

BOYCE, E. R. (1959) *The Gay Way Series*. London: Macmillan.

BREARLEY, M. and NEILSON, L. (1964) *Queensway Reading*. London: Evans.

BURROUGHS, G. E. R. (1957) *A Study of the Vocabulary of Young Children*. London: Oliver & Boyd.

CARVER, C. and STOWASSER, C. H. (1963) *Oxford Colour Reading Books*. Oxford: Oxford University Press.

CHALL, J. S. (1967) *Learning to Read: The Great Debate*. New York: McGraw-Hill.

CLYMER, T. (1963) 'The utility of phonic generalisations.' *The Reading Teacher*, Vol. 16, No. 4, pp. 252–258. Newark, Delaware: International Reading Association.

CLYMER, T. (1968) 'What is "reading" ?: some current concepts.' In ROBINSON, H. M. (ed.) *Innovation and Change in Reading Instruction*. The Sixty-seventh Yearbook of the National Society for the Study of Education, Part 2. Chicago: Chicago University Press.

CUISENAIRE, G. and GATTEGNO, C. (1954) *Numbers in Colour*. London: Heinemann.

CUTFORTH, J. A. and BATTERSBY, S. H. (1962) *Children and Books*. Oxford: Basil Blackwell.

DALE, N. (1899) *On the Teaching of English Reading*. London: Philip.

DANIELS, J. C. (1966) 'The place of phonics.' In DOWNING, J. A. (ed.) *The First International Reading Symposium, Oxford 1964*. London: Cassell.

DANIELS, J. C. and DIACK, H. (1954) *The Royal Road Readers*. London: Chatto & Windus.

DANIELS, J. C. and DIACK, H. (1956) *Progress in Reading*. Nottingham: University Institute of Education.

DANIELS, J. C. and DIACK, H. (1958) *Standard Reading Tests*. London: Chatto & Windus.

DANIELS, J. C. and DIACK, H. (1958) *Progress in Reading in the Infant School*. Nottingham: University Institute of Education.

DANIELS, J. C. and SEGAL, S. S. (1966)   *Help in Reading: Books for the Teaching of Backward Children and for Pupils Backward in Reading.* London: The National Book League.

DAVENPORT, P. (1953)   *Pilot Reading Scheme.* Leeds: E. J. Arnold.

DEAN, J. (1966)   'Words in Colour.' In DOWNING, J. A. (ed.) *The First International Reading Symposium, Oxford 1964.* London: Cassell.

DEAN, J. (1967)   'Second report on Words in Colour.' In DOWNING, J. A. and BROWN, A. L. (eds.) *The Second International Reading Symposium.* London: Cassell.

DEARDEN, R. F. (1968)   *The Philosophy of Primary Education.* London: Routledge & Kegan Paul.

DEPARTMENT OF EDUCATION AND SCIENCE (1967)   The Plowden Report: *Children and their Primary Schools, Vol. 1: The Report.* London: H. M. Stationery Office.

DEPARTMENT OF EDUCATION AND SCIENCE (1967)   The Plowden Report: *Children and their Primary Schools, Vol. 2: Research and Surveys.* Appendices 9, 10 and 11, pp. 347–594. London: H. M. Stationery Office.

DIACK, H. (1960)   *Reading and the Psychology of Perception.* Nottingham: Peter Skinner.

DIACK, H. (1965)   *In Spite of the Alphabet.* London: Chatto & Windus.

DOWNING, J. A. (1962)   *To Be or Not to Be: The New Augmented Roman Alphabet Explained and Illustrated.* London: Cassell.

DOWNING, J. A. (1963)   *The Downing Reading Scheme.* London: Initial Teaching Publishing Co.

DOWNING, J. A. (1964)   *The Initial Teaching Alphabet: Explained and Illustrated.* London: Cassell.

DOWNING: J. A. (1967a)   *The i.t.a. Symposium.* Slough: National Foundation for Educational Research.

DOWNING, J. A. (1967b)   *Evaluating the Initial Teaching Alphabet.* London: Cassell.

FLESCH, R. (1955)   *Why Johnny Can't Read.* New York: Harper & Row.

FRIES, C. C. (1962)   *Linguistics and Reading.* New York: Holt, Rinehart & Winston.

FRIES, C. C., WILSON, R. G., and RUDOLPH, M. K. (1966) *Merrill Linguistic Readers.* Columbus: Merrill.

FRY, E. B. (1966)   'First grade reading instruction using diacritical marking system, initial teaching alphabet and basal reading system.' *The Reading Teacher,* Vol. 19, No. 8, pp. 666–669. Newark, Delaware: International Reading Association.

FRY, E. B. (1967a)   'The diacritical marking system and a preliminary comparison with i.t.a.' In DOWNING, J. A. and BROWN, A. L. (eds.) *The Second International Reading Symposium,* London: Cassell.

FRY, E. B. (1967b)   'First grade reading instruction using diacritical marking system, initial teaching alphabet and basal reading system – extended to second grade.' *The Reading Teacher,* Vol. 20, No. 8, pp. 687–693. Newark, Delaware: International Reading Association.

FRY, E. B. (1967c) 'Comparison of beginning reading with i.t.a., d.m.s. and t.o. after three years.' *The Reading Teacher*, Vol. 22, No. 4, pp. 357–362. Newark, Delaware: International Reading Association.

GARDNER, D. E. M. and CASS, J. (1965) *The Role of the Teacher in the Infant and Nursery School.* Oxford: Pergamon.

GATES, A. I. (1935) *The Improvement of Reading.* New York: Macmillan.

GATTEGNO, C. (1962a) *Words in Colour.* Reading, Berks: Educational Explorers.

GATTEGNO, C. (1962b) *Words in Colour: Background and Principles.* Reading, Berks: Educational Explorers.

GATTEGNO, C. (1962c) *Words in Colour.* Teacher's Guide. Reading, Berks: Educational Explorers.

GATTEGNO, C. (1969) *Reading with Words in Colour: A Scientific Study of the Problems of Reading.* Reading, Berks: Educational Explorers.

GEORGIADES, N. J. (1969) *The Initial Teaching Alphabet in Remedial Reading Groups.* London: Harrap.

GODDARD, N. L. (1958, revised edition 1969) *Reading in the Modern Infants' School.* London: University of London Press.

GOODACRE, E. J. (1967) *Reading in Infant Classes. Teaching Beginners to Read,* Report No. 1. Slough: National Foundation for Educational Research.

GOODACRE, E. J. (1968) *Teachers and their Pupils' Home Background.* Slough: National Foundation for Educational Research.

GRASSAM, E. H. (1965) *Six Phonic Workbooks.* London: Ginn.

GRAY, W. S. (1956) *The Teaching of Reading and Writing – An International Survey.* London: Evans.

GRAY, W. S., MONROE, M., ARTLEY, A. S., and ARBUTHNOT, M. H. (1956) *The Happy Trio Reading Scheme.* Exeter: Wheaton.

HARRISON, M. (1964) *Instant Reading: The Story of the Initial Teaching Alphabet.* London: Pitman.

HARRISON, J. (1966) *Oldham Readers.* London: Initial Teaching Publishing Co.

JONES, W. R. (1965) *Step up and Read.* London: University of London Press.

JONES, J. K. (1965) 'Colour as an aid to visual perception in early reading.' *British Journal of Educational Psychology*, Vol. 35, No. 1, pp. 22–27.

JONES, J. K. (1967a) *Colour Story Reading: A Research Report.* London: Nelson.

JONES, J. K. (1967b) *Colour Story Reading.* London: Nelson.

JONES, J. K. (1968a) 'Phonetic colour reading.' In DOWNING, J. A. and BROWN, A. L. (eds.) *The Third International Reading Symposium.* London: Cassell.

JONES, J. K. (1968b) 'Comparing i.t.a. with Colour Story Reading.' *Educational Research*, Vol. 10, No. 3, pp. 226–234.

JONES, J. K. (1969) 'Reading in colour'. *The Guardian*, January 24th.

KAMM, A. and TAYLOR, B. (1966) *Books and The Teacher.* London: University of London Press.

KEIR, G. (1947a) *Adventures in Writing.* Oxford: Oxford University Press.

KEIR, G. (1947b) *Adventures in Reading.* Oxford: Oxford University Press.

KERFOOT, J. F. (1965) *First Grade Reading Programmes.* Newark, Delaware: Internationa Reading Association.

LAWSON, K. S. (1968) *Children's Reading,* Paper No. 8. Leeds: University Institute of Education.

LEE, T. (1967) 'Writing the talking: an appraisal of Words in Colour.' In BROWN, A. L. *Reading: Current Research and Practice,* Vol. 1. Edinburgh: Chambers.

LEIGH, T. (1967) *i.t.a. in the Classroom.* Edinburgh: Chambers.

MAZURKIEWICZ, E. J. and TANYZER, H. J. (1963) *Early to Read Series.* New York: i.t.a. Publications Inc.

MCCULLAGH, S. K. (1959) *Griffin Readers.* Leeds: Arnold.

MCKEE, P., HARRISON, M. L., MCCOWAN, A., LEHR, E. (1956) *The McKee Readers.* London: Nelson.

MCNALLY, J. and MURRAY, W. (1962) *Key Words to Literacy.* London: The Schoolmaster Publishing Co.

MELSER, J. (1960) *Read it Yourself Books.* London: Methuen.

MILES, J. E. (1951) *Active Reading.* London: Ginn.

MINISTRY OF EDUCATION (1950) *Reading Ability: Some Suggestions for Helping the Backward,* Pamphlet No. 18. London: H. M. Stationery Office.

MINISTRY OF EDUCATION (1957) *Standards of Reading 1948–1956,* Pamphlet No. 32. London: H. M. Stationery Office.

MINISTRY OF EDUCATION (1959) *Primary Education.* London: H. M. Stationery Office.

MORRIS, J. M. (1966) *Standards and Progress in Reading.* Slough: National Foundation for Educational Research.

MORRIS, R. (1963) *Success and Failure in Learning to Read.* London: Oldbourne.

MOUNTFORD, J. (1964) *Short Notes for Reference on i.t.a. Transliteration.* Edinburgh: Chambers.

MOUNTFORD, J. (1965) *i.t.a. as a Grading Device. Reading Research Document No. 5.* Edinburgh: Chambers.

MOXON, C. A. V. (1962) *A Remedial Reading Method.* London: Methuen.

MOYLE, D. (1968) *The Teaching of Reading.* London: Ward Lock.

MURPHY, Sister Mary Leonore (1968a) *Douglas Can't Read.* Reading, Berks: Educational Explorers.

MURPHY, Sister Mary Leonore (1968b) *Barnaby: The Struggle of a Word-blind Boy.* Reading, Berks: Educational Explorers.

MURRAY, W. (1964) *Key Words Reading Scheme.* Loughborough: Wills & Hepworth.

NEALE, N. D. (1958) *Analysis of Reading Ability.* London: Macmillan.

OBRIST, C. and PICKARD, P. M. (1967) *Time for Reading.* London: Ginn.

O'DONNELL, M. and MUNRO, R. (1949) *Janet and John.* Welwyn: Nisbet.

O'DONNELL, M. and MUNRO, R. (1956) *High on a Hill. Days in the Sun. The Five-and-a-Half Club.* Welwyn: Nisbet.

PARKER, D. H. (1958) *The S. R. A. Reading Laboratories.* Chicago: Science Research Associates.

PASCOE, T. W. (ed.) (1962) *A Second Survey of Books for Backward Readers.* London: University of London Press.

PIERS, H. (1966) *Mouse Books.* London: Methuen.

PITMAN, J. (1959) *The Ernhardt Augmented (40-sound 42-character) Lower-case Roman Alphabet.* London: Pitman.

PITMAN, J. (1961) 'Learning to read: an experiment'. *Journal of Royal Society of Arts,* Vol. 109, pp. 149–180.

PULLEN, A. and RAPSTOFF, C. (1967) *Inner Ring Books.* London: Benn.

RANDELL, B. and MCDONALD, J. (1968) *Methuen Caption Books.* London: Methuen.

REIS, M. (1962) *Fun with Phonics.* Cambridge: Cambridge Arts Publishers.

ROBERTS, G. R. (1969) *Reading in Primary Schools.* London: Routledge & Kegan Paul.

ROBERTS, G. R. and LUNZER, E. A. (1968) 'Reading and learning to read.' In LUNZER, E. A. and MORRIS, J. F. (eds.) *Development in Human Learning.* London: Staples.

SCEATS, J. (1967) *i.t.a. and the Teaching of Literacy.* London: The Bodley Head.

SCHONELL, F. J. and SERJEANT, I. (1939) *Happy Venture Readers.* Edinburgh: Oliver & Boyd.

SCHONELL, F. J. (1942) *Backwardness in the Basic Subjects.* Edinburgh: Oliver & Boyd.

SCHONELL, F. J. (1945) *The Psychology and Teaching of Reading.* London: Oliver & Boyd.

SCHONELL, F. J. (1945) *Graded Word Reading Test.* London: Oliver & Boyd.

SCHONELL, F. J. and FLOWERDEW, P. (1953) *The Wide Range Readers.* Edinburgh: Oliver & Boyd.

SIMPSON, M. (1966) *Ready to Read.* London: Methuen.

SOUTHGATE, V. (1968a) *First Words.* London: Macmillan.

SOUTHGATE, V. (1968b) 'Formulae for beginning reading tuition.' *Educational Research,* Vol. 11, pp. 23–30.

SOUTHGATE, V. and HAVENHAND, J. (1959) *Sounds and Words.* London: University of London Press.

STONES, E. (1967) *An Introduction to Educational Psychology.* London: Methuen.

STOTT, D. H. (1960) *Micky Books.* Oxford: Blackwell.

STOTT, D. H. (1961) *Day of the Week Books.* Glasgow: Holmes.

STOTT, D. H. (1962) *Programmed Reading Kit.* Glasgow: Holmes.

STOTT, D. H. (1964) *Roads to Literacy.* Glasgow: Holmes.

TANSLEY, A. E. (1961) *Sound Sense.* Leeds: Arnold.

TAYLOR, J. and INGLEBY, T. (1960) *Let's Learn to Read.* London: Blackie.

TAYLOR, J. and INGLEBY, T. (1965) *This is the Way I Go.* London: Longmans.

TUDOR-HART, B. (1969) *An Experiment in Teaching Method Using i.t.a., 1964–68.* (unpublished report). London: i.t.a. Foundation.

VERNON, M. D. (1962) *The Psychology of Perception.* Harmondsworth: Penguin.

WARBURTON, F. W. and SOUTHGATE, V. (1969) *i.t.a.: An Independent Evaluation.* Edinburgh: Chambers, and London: Murray.

WISEMAN, S. (1964) *Education and Environment.* Manchester: Manchester University Press.

WISEMAN, S. (1967) 'The Manchester survey.' The Plowden Report: *Children and their Primary Schools, Vol. 2: Research and Surveys,* Appendix 9, pp. 349–400. London: H.M. Stationery Office.

WITTICK, M. L. (1968) 'Innovations in reading instruction for beginners.' In ROBINSON, H. M. (ed.) *Innovation and Change in Reading Instruction.* The Sixty-seventh Yearbook of the National Society for the Study of Education, Part 2. Chicago: Chicago University Press.

Appendix

The Vocabulary of Five Look-and-say Reading Schemes

Table B.1. Key Words Reading Scheme
(Murray, W., 1964)

BOOK		NEW WORDS	PHONIC BOOK	ADDITIONAL PHONIC WORDS
Infant	1a	16	1c	4
Stage	2a	27	2c	—
	3a	36	3c	—
	4a	41	4c	21
	5a	46	5c	42
	6a	52	6c	39
	7a	67	7c	64
	8a	92	8c	70
	9a	110	9c	99
Totals		487		339
Junior	10a	115	10c	125
Stage	11a	138	11c	288
	12a	140	12c	(not given)
Totals		880		752+

It should be noted that new sight words are introduced in the 'a' books and they are repeated in the 'b' books. The 'c' books incorporate written exercises and introduce phonic words and rules.

Table B.2.   Happy Venture Reading Scheme
(Schonell, F. J. and Serjeant I., 1939)

BASIC BOOKS	NEW WORDS	PLAY BOOKS	NEW WORDS	TOTAL NO. OF NEW WORDS
Introductory	44	Introductory	35	79
1	62	1	70	132
2	103	2	75	178
3	210	3	64	274
4	384	4	117	501
Totals	803		361	1164

Table B.3.   Queensway Reading
(Brearley, M. and Neilson, L., 1964)

BOOK	NEW WORDS	ADDITIONAL WORDS IN COMPLEMENTARY BOOKS				TOTAL NO. OF NEW WORDS
		a	b	c	d	
1	59	7	11	15	13	105
2	42	7	6	6	6	67
3	70	9	13	13	20	125
4	123	35	20	29	49	256
5	206	32	40	—	—	278
6	210	60	77	—	—	347

Total 1178

It should be noted that three additional books have been published since the teacher's manual was written but, as no indication is given of the number of new words introduced in these books, they are not included in the above table.

Table B.4. Janet and John (Whole-word Course)

(O'Donnell, M. and Munro, R., 1949)

BOOK	NEW WORDS
1. Here We Go	27
2. Off to Play	32
3. Out and About	46
4. I Went Walking	84
5. Through the Garden Gate	230
6. I Know a Story	359
7. Once Upon a Time	423
	Total 1201

It should be noted that the numbers of words given in the above table refer only to the Janet and John *Whole-word Course; they do not apply to the parallel* Janet and John *courses known as the Phonic Course and the Modified Phonic Course.*

Table B.5. Time for Reading

(Obrist, C., and Pickard, P. M., 1967)

The complete reading scheme consists of a progression of apparatus and books falling into thirty sections. As certain of the new words are introduced through apparatus and others in the eighteen books forming part of the scheme, it would be unrealistic to attempt to isolate the new words introduced in the books alone. Accordingly, the figures given in the following table refer to the vocabulary of the entire scheme.

SECTIONS	NO. OF BOOKS	NEW WORDS
1– 5	1	88
6–16	7	197
17–27	7	285
28–30	3	1145
		Total 1715

Index